# Easy Guide to
# Sewing Skirts

Marcy Tilton

The Taunton Press

Cover Photo: Boyd Hagan
Back Cover Photos: Robert Marsala

Designer: Jodie Delohery
Layout Artist: Catherine Cassidy
Illustrator: Steve Buchanan
Typeface: Bookman/Optima
Paper: 70 lb. Warren Patina Matte
Printer: Quebecor Printing Hawkins, New Canton, Tennessee

## Taunton
BOOKS & VIDEOS

*for fellow enthusiasts*

First printing: 1995
Second printing: 1996
Printed in the United States of America

A THREADS Book
THREADS® is a trademark of The Taunton Press, Inc.,
registered in the U.S. Patent and Trademark Office.

The Taunton Press, 63 South Main Street, Box 5506,
Newtown, CT 06470-5506

Library of Congress Cataloging-in-Publication Data

Tilton, Marcy.
    Easy guide to sewing skirts / Marcy Tilton.
       p.  cm.
    Includes index.
    ISBN 1-56158-088-0
    1. Skirts.  2. Sewing.  I. Title.
TT540.T55  1995
646.4´3504--dc20              95-6384
                        CIP

# Introduction

I have sewn hundreds, maybe thousands, of garments during a 35-year career that has been devoted to this pleasurable passion of mine. But the garment that stands out most clearly in my mind is the very first one I made.

I was 16 years old, loved beautiful clothes, and haunted Frank Murphy's, St. Paul, Minnesota's finest women's store, where I found the garment that inspired me—a lemon-yellow Irish linen straight skirt. Simple. Sophisticated. The $110 price tag was clearly beyond me, so I found the fabric and sewed a copy of the skirt in a weekend. I was amazed at how quickly things came together, elated at what fun this was and how good it felt to create just what I wanted from a bit of fabric, a pattern, and some thread. I was hooked.

I had my first clothing class a few years later in college. Starting once more with a skirt—a supple, moss-green, wide-wale-corduroy A-line, cut on the bias—I learned about fitting, pressing, lining, making the inside as beautiful as the outside. I wore that skirt out, shortening it each year as the mini-skirt gradually emerged on the scene.

I learned to sew from nuns who taught with gentle kindness and good humor (I wondered how they had learned all this—they wore the same thing every day!) as well as from my beloved Aunt Mary who fixed my mistakes, ripped when I was discouraged, and predicted: "You will never be able to walk past a fabric store again."

Years later, I met Sandra Betzina, who had a school in San Francisco devoted to fashion sewing, and I thought I had died and gone to heaven. I taught classes for her and on my own throughout the Bay Area. A few years after Sandra closed her school, my school, The Sewing Workshop, the fulfillment of my dream, was born.

Since then, I have learned from my colleagues, from tailors and dressmakers, from fabric artists, from students, from books and videos, from classes, and from keeping a close eye on ready-to-wear. The information in this book is the result of a lifetime of seeking knowledge, trial and error, success and failure. I have learned to appreciate "mistakes" because, through them, new techniques, ideas, and improvements develop.

Through teaching and communicating about sewing, clothes, and fashion, I continue to learn and grow. I hope that your creative journey will bring you as much pleasure and satisfaction as it has brought me, from the day I made that yellow skirt.

# 1 *Which Skirt to Make?*

Anyone can sew a skirt, so if you're just learning, a skirt is the perfect starting point. You can get the color, style, and fit you want, and the length that's exactly right for you.

The number of choices in the pattern books may seem overwhelming at first, but there are really only a few skirt styles and silhouettes to choose from. In this chapter, you'll learn how to determine which styles work best on your figure and which styles and fabrics are best for your skill level.

A simple style and a beautiful fabric are the best combination for fast, easy, and successful sewing (just look at the skirts in any Calvin Klein collection). When you want to make a skirt quickly, stay at or just below your skill level and use the techniques and details that you've mastered. If you want to stretch your limits, choose skirts with some new element—a different zipper application, a more fitted style, or a more challenging fabric.

The more difficult and time-consuming skirts to sew are those that are fitted at the waist, high hip, and full hip, or that have more pattern pieces and construction details, such as pleats or pockets.

# Choosing the Best Style

*Begin in your closet. Try on your favorite skirts. Make notes and take measurements.*

Decide which styles and silhouettes look best on you. What are the most flattering lengths? Which waistband styles, lengths, and widths are most comfortable? What is the hip measurement of the fitted skirt that looks best on you?

Next, take your tape measure to the stores. Try on a variety of skirts to see what works for you and what doesn't. (I do this at least twice a year—late August and March are when the stores have the best seasonal selections.) Again, make notes of the most flattering lengths, hem widths, waistbands, and so on. Check the fabric types—this will help you learn which fabrics work best for which styles. If you find a skirt in the stores that looks fabulous on you, you'll probably be able to find something similar in the pattern books.

## What's Best for Me?

Skirt styles fall into a few basic categories: straight, A-line or flared, gored, pleated/tucked, gathered, wrap, and bias. But how well a particular style will look on you depends on your figure type. Some styles look good on almost anyone, while others seem to suit a particular body shape. The so-called "average" or slim, well-proportioned figure can wear almost any style of skirt. Four of the other common figure types and the styles that most flatter them are described on the facing page.

The chart on pp.10-13 describes each of the basic skirt styles, the figure type best suited to each, the range of sewing skills required, and the recommended fabrics. For easy reference, each skirt style is coded with the appropriate figure symbols. The page numbers in parentheses direct you to more detailed discussion of the suggested style variations and design details.

# FIGURE TYPES

**X or Hourglass**  The hourglass figure looks balanced, curvaceous, and well defined. The shoulders and hips appear to be the same width, and the bust and hips are about 10 in. to 12 in. larger than the waist (an hourglass figure might measure 38-27-38, for example). A woman with this shape can wear both straight and flared styles. If you're full figured, however, you'll look better with straight lines that minimize your curves, such as those on a skirt with vertical seams.

**A or Pear**  On a pear-shaped figure, the shoulders appear narrower than the hips or thighs, the bust is small, and the waist is small in proportion to the hips. If you are pear shaped—most women are—avoid bulky skirts and severe slim-line skirts. Flared, A-line, gored, and bias skirts are most flattering. To camouflage full hips, choose soft, flowing fabrics, soft pleats, and long, graceful skirts.

**H or Rectangular**  The rectangular figure has few curves and not much waistline definition. The shoulders and the hips are similar in width, which makes the figure appear balanced. If you have a rectangular shape, most likely your clothes usually hang well. You can wear skirts that are slim-fitting, as well as ones that are graceful and flowing.

**Y or Wedge**  The wedge figure has shoulders that are broader than the hips, and the upper arms may be heavy. Some women develop a wedge shape as they age; others are born with these proportions. If you have a wedge shape, slim skirts are made for you. Gored and bias skirts are also good choices.

Hourglass figure

Pear figure

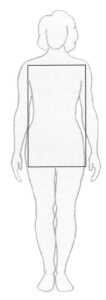

Rectangular figure

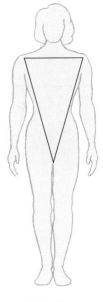

Wedge figure

# STYLES, SKILLS, AND FABRICS

| Skirt types | Style and figure notes | Required skills | Suggested fabrics |
|---|---|---|---|
| **STRAIGHT**<br><br>☒ ■ ▼<br><br>A straight skirt is cut straight (or tapers in slightly) from the full hip to the hem.<br><br>[skirt illustration] | More than any other style, straight skirts reveal the figure. An oversized top worn over a straight skirt, however, works well on figures with proportionally large hips.<br><br>Short straight skirts ending just above the knee are the most flattering. Super-short straight skirts, such as the micro-mini, are best on slim, long-legged figures.<br><br>Long straight skirts can have an air of chic, but look dowdy if they're the wrong length. They're best if they end where the leg begins to taper.<br><br>Some French designers use patterns that are slightly "pegged" at the hem—cut about ½ in. narrower than the full hip at each side seam. A pegged skirt tapers from full hip to hem, creating a curvy, pleasing line for almost any figure that can wear a slim skirt. | Straight skirts fit closer to the body than any other style, so it's important to have some experience with fitting.<br><br>A traditional tailored straight skirt might have darts, soft pleats, curved seams, a zipper, fitted waistband, vent or kick pleat, and a lining.<br><br>**Easy:** A slim skirt with a pull-on elasticized waistband (pp. 89-91) is an ideal beginner's project. A French vent (p. 72) and lining (pp. 82-85) are optional.<br><br>**Average:** Soft front pleats (pp. 61-63); darts (p. 59), gathers (pp. 64-65), or elastic (pp. 96-98) in the back; machine-stitched zipper (pp. 78-79) at center-back seam; optional French vent (p. 72) and lining (pp. 82-85).<br><br>**Advanced:** Darts (pp. 59-60) in front and back; shaped darts for better fit or pockets (pp.66-69); hand-picked zipper (p. 79); lining (pp. 82-85). | For fitted, darted styles, the best fabrics are midweight, sometimes termed "bottom weights" that is, for skirts or pants.<br><br>The best choices in wools are crepe, lightweight gabardine, fine tweeds, and twills. Avoid wool flannel; most kinds are too stiff and heavy for any skirt.<br><br>Other fabrics that work well are linens, silk linen or blends, light tweeds, brushed cottons, and denim-weight cottons.<br><br>For pull-on straight skirts, fabrics should be soft and fluid to avoid excess bulk at the waist and high hip. Silks, wool jersey, challis, and rayon are good choices. |

| Skirt type | Style and figure notes | Required skills | Suggested fabrics |
|---|---|---|---|
| **A-LINE/FLARED**<br><br>⧖ ■ ▲<br><br>An A-line skirt is fuller at the hem than at the waist.<br><br> | The A-line or flared skirt is probably the best style for most women. It works well on figures with a small waist in proportion to the hips; adds the illusion of a waist on straight up-and-down figures; and may be the only style that works on full-hipped figures.<br><br>Check the shapes of the pattern pieces on the instruction sheet. The skirt should be flared, not rectangular. If the lengthwise grain is at center back or front, you may want to alter it for a more flattering effect.<br><br>Also check the finished skirt width at the hem to be sure it's exactly what you want, based on the measurements you've taken of garments in your wardrobe or in stores. | A-line skirts may be fitted at the waist, high hip, and full hip, which requires skill in fitting. They can also be full with an elasticized waistband—super-easy to sew and fit.<br><br>**Easy:** Full skirt with pull-on elasticized waistband (pp. 89-91); gathers (pp. 64-65) or soft pleats (p. 61); machine-sewn hem (pp. 106-107).<br><br>**Average:** Fitted or partially elasticized waistband (pp. 96-98); zipper (pp. 74-81); pocket detailing (pp. 66-69); curved seams (p. 53).<br><br>**Advanced:** Bias cut (pp. 37-39); lining (pp. 82-83); raised waistband (p.101); more fitted, but the more fitted the skirt, the more skills are required to make it. | Because A-line skirts are usually flowing, choose fabrics that drape and move nicely.<br><br>For more fitted styles, choose wool crepe, double knits, light gabardine, rayon and silk tweed, brushed denim, suede, silk linen.<br><br>For full, gathered, or softly pleated flared styles, pick silk broadcloth, crepe de chine, rayon, challis, tissue faille, cotton knits, silk noil, wool jersey. |

| Skirt type | Style and figure notes | Required skills | Suggested fabrics |
|---|---|---|---|
| **GORED**<br>☒ ■ ▲ ▼<br><br>This style consists of four, six, eight, or more gores shaped to flare from waist to hem.<br><br> | A true classic, the gored skirt is always in fashion. It's also one of the most flattering styles. The vertical lines of a gored skirt create an illusion of height and slimness.<br><br>A gored skirt can be either straight or A-line, depending on the contours of the gores. If you look best in a slim skirt, choose a gored style that's fitted at the waist and hips and that flares near the hemline. If an A-line is best for you, choose a skirt with gores that flare from waist or high hip. Shaped and curvy gores emphasize the hips.<br><br>(See pp. 108-109 for tips on constructing a fitted, lightly fitted, and full gored skirt.) | The more fitted the skirt, the more important your fitting ability. You'll also need accurate stitching and pressing skills to achieve flat, nearly invisible seams. Hems can be sewn by hand or machine.<br><br>**Easy:** Pull-on elasticized waistband (pp. 89-91); additional ease at waist and hips (p.108).<br><br>**Average:** Lightly fitted skirt (p. 108); invisible zipper (pp. 80-81); machine-topstitched hem (p. 106)<br><br>**Advanced:** Fitted (p. 109); hand-picked or invisible zipper (p. 79 and pp. 80-81); hand-sewn hem (p. 105). | The best fabrics for this style are fluid and drapey.<br><br>Wool jersey, velour, and wool double knits are good for lightly fitted skirts; wool crepe, silk tweed, and fine worsted wool for fitted skirts. Silk crepe de chine and rayon are also good choices.<br><br>Avoid wool flannel and gabardine. |

| Skirt type | Style and figure notes | Required skills | Suggested fabrics |
|---|---|---|---|
| **PLEATED/TUCKED**<br><br>■ ▼<br><br>You can vary the size, number and placement of the pleats to create different effects. | Pleats create a subtle vertical line while softening the figure. A skirt with all-around pleats, however, flatters only slim, narrow-hipped figures.<br><br>The position, direction, and depth of the pleats can be varied from those on the pattern to achieve the look that's best for you. Experiment. | **Easy:** Soft pleats (p. 61).<br><br>**Average:** Pressed-down or stitched-down pleats (pp. 62-63).<br><br>**Advanced:** All-around pleats, which are extremely difficult to fit. | Soft pleats require soft fabrics, such as silk and silkies, rayon, and jersey.<br><br>The best choices for pressed- or stitched-down pleats are crisp fabrics, such as light gabardine and menswear worsteds, silk twill, and broadcloth. |
| **GATHERED**<br><br>⧗ ▲<br><br>Gathers emphasize the drape and movement of soft, fluid fabrics. | Gathered skirts visually add weight and bulk to any figure, so choose your pattern and fabric carefully.<br><br>Beware the rectangular-shaped "dirndl" skirt, which is fine for children but frumpy on most women. Check the pattern instruction sheet to make sure the pattern pieces are narrower at the waist than at the hem.<br><br>Carefully position the gathers (pp. 64-65) for the most flattering effect. | Beginners often choose to make a gathered skirt as a first project, but gathers take patience and fussing to get just right.<br><br>**Easy:** Gathers created by an elasticized waistband (p. 89); short spans of gathers.<br><br>**Average/Advanced:** Long spans of gathers; a multi-tiered, Santa Fe–style skirt. | To avoid an unflattering puffy look, use soft, fluid fabrics, such as silk, polyester "silkies," rayon, jersey, and challis.<br><br>If you're unsure whether a fabric is too heavy for a gathered skirt, it probably is. |

# Selecting the Pattern

*Keep it simple. The key to success is to begin with a loose-fitting style and a beautiful fabric.*

As a rule, a garment with fewer pattern pieces requires less time to fit and sew. Scrutinize the illustrations in the pattern books. Keep in mind that each detail—yokes, pockets, pleats, raised waistbands, and intricate seam treatments—adds time and complexity to the project.

Build your skills gradually. With each new garment you make, plan to add another technique or fitting skill to your repertoire. For instance, once you've made a simple, slim skirt with an elastic waistband and a machine-stitched hem, you may want to make the same pattern again, this time adding pockets to the side seams and hand-stitching the hem. Then you'll be ready for a more challenging pattern, say, a darted skirt with a kick pleat and a fitted waistband.

## Beyond the Pattern Envelope

The pattern envelope contains a lot of useful information, but you have to know how to interpret it. Pattern illustrations can be somewhat misleading, because the artists' drawings are much taller and slimmer than most real women actually are. So keep in mind that you'll probably look very different in the skirt than the figure in the sketch. Also, if there's a photograph of a designer original, remember that the pattern company does not buy the original pattern, but rather the right to copy the design, so the cut of the garment won't be exactly the same.

Don't get distracted by details, such as a skirt pocket or the color of the garment in the illustration. Look at the lines of the drawings on the back of the pattern envelope. These will show you the skirt's basic silhouette—that is, whether it is straight, flared, or gathered.

Open the envelope, if the retailer will allow you to, and check the line drawing on the pattern instruction sheet. This is usually larger than the one on the pattern envelope, and the details are easier to see. Also check the shape and grainline position of the pattern pieces.

Check the finished skirt length and width, and compare these to your notes on what looks best on you. Your best lengths may vary, too, depending on the style of the skirt. Length is simple to change, but widths are more difficult to adjust, so you may need to try another size.

Read through the pattern instructions. Be sure you understand or can learn every step. Check the garment details to be sure you are confident you can master them. If not, see if you can simplify the skirt, at least the first time you make it.

## Which Size to Buy?

Choose a skirt pattern based on your full-hip measurement (p. 28), not your waist measurement—the waistline is easier to adjust than the hip. If your upper thighs are larger than your hips (as on a pear-shaped figure), substitute your upper-thigh measurement for the hip measurement when selecting the size.

If the skirt is part of an ensemble pattern, select the pattern size you would normally take in a blouse or jacket. You don't have to buy another pattern for the skirt—simply adjust the skirt pattern to fit. It's much easier to alter a skirt than it is to alter a blouse or a jacket.

While you're searching the pattern books for a skirt, be sure to also check the patterns that show ensembles. You just might find the perfect skirt, as well as a matching jacket or coat.

# 2 Working with Fabrics

It's impossible to select fabric without touching it. When you find a fabric that appeals to you, open it out to the length of the garment to examine its drape and overall effect. Crush it in your hand to see if it wrinkles and if the creases disappear easily. Take the bolt to a full-length mirror and hold the fabric up against you, draping it like a skirt. Stand back and squint to get a different perspective—sometimes a fabric that's appealing at close range isn't when you see it from a distance.

If your skirt will have pleats, fold the fabric to duplicate them. If you want to make a skirt with gathers, scrunch up the fabric to imitate a gathered effect. From these tests, you'll discover whether the fabric drapes smoothly and gracefully (which will flatter the figure without adding bulk) or is stiff and three-dimensional.

When you begin shopping, the fabrics recommended on the back of the pattern envelope are a good starting point. These are the fabrics the pattern designer believes will work best for that garment. Often these recommendations are too generic, however, and make no allowances for the sewer's abilities. The recommendations also fail to take into account that the characteristics of a specific fabric type (such as wool gabardine) can vary greatly. Consult the chart on pp. 10-13 for other suggested fabrics for your skirt style.

# A Glossary of Fashion Fabrics

*Allow yourself time to select just the right fabric—one that you will enjoy sewing and wearing.*

The most common mistake that sewers make is to pair a pattern with an incompatible fabric. If a fabric seems too heavy, too slippery, too wrinkly, too unstable, prone to fraying, or not quite the right color, keep looking. Most sewers have a "little voice" inside that instinctively recognizes when a fabric isn't acceptable. Better to find out before the garment is made than during the project or, worse yet, after the skirt is finished. When you're not sure how a fabric will handle, buy 1/8 yd. to experiment with.

# Foolproof Fabrics

Certain fabrics are like dependable old friends. They are a pleasure to touch, gratifying to sew and press, and they wear, move, and flow beautifully. Natural fibers head the list of foolproof fabrics for skirts.

**Cotton:** *Denim, brushed cotton, chambray, fine poplin, lawn.* Look for long-fiber cottons (the best quality), which can be identified by their beautiful sheen and resistance to wrinkles. A pleasure to sew and press, these cottons last and last.

**Wool:** *Wool crepe, double knits, wool jersey (though not for rank beginners), wool challis.* The weight and drape of wool makes it a perfect skirt fabric. Wool crepe is excellent, as the texture does not add bulk to the figure. It's also easy to press and sew. Avoid wool flannel entirely—it's thick and bulky and doesn't press well.

**Linen:** *Linen blends.* Linen blends well with other fibers. With linen/rayon, for example, you get the best of both fabrics—the drape of rayon and the stability of linen. Moygashel, a brand-name Irish linen, doesn't wrinkle as much as other pure linens. For slim and fitted flared skirts, choose heavy weights. Consider lining your linen skirt, depending on the style.

**Silk:** *Silk linen, silk noil, silk tweed, silk broadcloth.* Silk can be smooth and slippery or have the look and feel of cotton or linen. Until you have more experience, avoid the slippery silks, such as charmeuse, crepe de chine, georgette, and chiffon.

## NEEDLES, THREADS, AND STITCHES

For most skirt fabrics (lightweight to midweight wovens and some knits), a #12/80 universal-point needle is best. With these fabrics, use a good-quality long-staple polyester thread and a 2mm to 2.5mm stitch length (about 8 to 10 stitches per inch).

For very lightweight fabric, such as crepe de chine, use a smaller needle (#10/70) and finer thread machine-embroidery thread, for example.

With heavy, dense, thick, or textured fabrics, use a longer stitch and larger needle. With denim, for example, use a #14/90 needle. Even if your fabric isn't heavy, because you are stitching through so many thicknesses, you may want to topstitch with a size #14/90 or special topstitching needle.

I baste with silk thread to avoid making indentations in the fabric when I press it before the final stitching.

*The feel, weight, and drape of the fabric are essential to the success of your finished garment.*

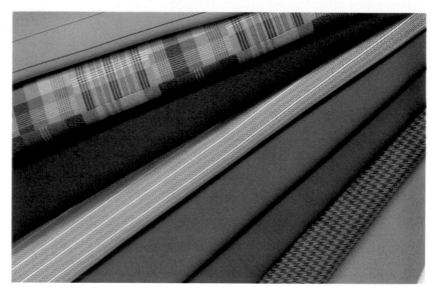

# Challenging Fabrics

Some fabrics are more challenging to work with because they require expertise in cutting, handling, sewing, pressing, and hand-stitching. To gain some experience gradually, combine a challenging fabric with a simple-to-construct design. For example, try making a simple four-gore pull-on skirt in rayon or silk crepe de chine.

**Rayon:** *A man-made fiber composed of natural materials.* Rayon's soft and drapey characteristics, which give the fabric its appeal, are also what can make it hard to handle. Sand-washed rayons, especially, shift and move easily while they are being cut and sewn. Imported, cottonlike rayons are often more stable and easier to handle than inexpensive, domestic versions. Try the wrinkle test: If the wrinkles fall out after you crumple the fabric, the rayon is probably of good quality and will be easier to sew.

**Polyester:** *A man-made fiber that can look and feel like silk or rayon.* Polyester is difficult to cut, sew, press, and shape. The fiber is so strong that topstitching often puckers. Avoid polyester "silkies" until you're a seasoned sewer, and even then, test the fabric first.

**Wool gabardine:** *Can be firm and crisp or soft and drapey.* Although suitable for a variety of skirt styles, gabardine is a difficult fabric for a beginner to work with because it eases poorly, frays readily, and shows stitching errors. Gabardine also requires expert pressing and topstitching to look its best.

# FABRICS FOR POCKETS, INTERFACINGS, AND LININGS

Once you've found your skirt fabric, select the fabrics for the other items you'll include in the skirt.

**Pockets:** If the skirt fabric is lightweight, doesn't show through from the right side, and won't stick to itself, make the pockets from the same fabric. You can also use the lining fabric to make the pockets.

Pockets may also be made of any strong, slippery fabric or plain-weave cotton in a color close to that of the skirt. Plain broadcloth or cotton twill are also good to use.

If the skirt fabric is a pale color or white, make the pockets of a lightweight lining fabric of nude- or flesh-toned silk or nylon organza.

**Interfacing:** You have a number of choices for waistband interfacing. You don't have to use what the pattern says. Although designed for shirt collars and

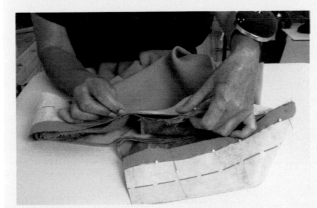

*Fusible interfacing creates a stable, crisp waistband.*

cuffs, woven fusible is perfect for waistbands. It creates a crisp finish that holds the waistband's shape. Sew-in interfacing doesn't work as well. There are also waistband styles for which you don't need interfacing (pp. 89-91).

**Lining:** A lining fabric should be thin, strong, and smooth. It should also be compatible with the weight, drape, and care requirements of the skirt fabric. The color should not be visible through the skirt fabric.

If your skirt pattern doesn't include a lining, you need to calculate how much fabric you should buy. The general rule is: double the skirt length. However, it's safer to lay out your pattern pieces on the lining fabric (except for the waistband, which is unlined). For future reference, note on the pattern envelope how much lining fabric you need for the skirt.

Rayon linings are ideal. Not only are they inexpensive, they "breathe" and have excellent draping qualities. They can be difficult to find, however. (Polyester, though less expensive and more available, doesn't breathe well and has only fair draping qualities.)

Silk is the ultimate in luxury. It's expensive, feels marvelous, and can add warmth to the garment. Crepe de chine is an excellent and sumptuous companion to wool crepe or light gabardine. China silk is an excellent traditional lining fabric, but beware of the thin, cheap varieties—with any stress at all (as in a fitted skirt), the seams may pull out.

| Pockets | Waistband Interfacings | Linings |
| --- | --- | --- |
| Plain-weave cotton | Fusible nonwoven, precut | Rayon |
| Plain broadcloth | Fusible woven yardage | Silk |
| Cotton twill | Sew-in woven, by the roll | Crepe de chine |
| Lining fabrics of silk or nylon organza | Elastic and flat-ribbed elastic | China silk |

# Preparing the Fabric

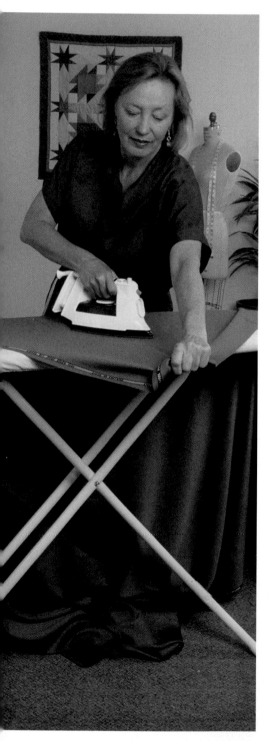

*Prepare the fabric before you sew to ensure that the finished garment will look, hang, and wear well.*

Most fabric will shrink the first time it's laundered, so you should wash or dry-clean it before you cut out the pattern pieces. Preshrink using the same method you plan to use to launder your finished skirt. For example, if you'll be washing and drying the skirt by machine, pretreat the fabric by machine. After preshrinking, straighten the grain of the fabric by pulling or pressing to ensure that the finished garment will look its best.

## Preshrinking and Pressing

Washing by hand is often the best way to launder hand-sewn garments. To preshrink the fabric, either wash and dry it by machine this first time only, or wash it by hand. To preshrink by hand, fold the fabric and submerge it in warm to hot water and a little detergent. (The detergent removes the excess dye or finishing substance.) Then rinse and air-dry the fabric.

Undyed white and off-white wools tend to shrink at alarming rates and should always be preshrunk. Lay the fabric on a large terry towel that has just been washed in the machine (the towel should be damp, not sodden). Roll the fabric and damp towel together like a jelly roll, leave them overnight, and, the next day, press the fabric smooth to remove the moisture.

Some fabrics, such as wool crepe, must be dry cleaned. To preshrink the fabric, have the dry cleaner process the piece of fabric just as if it were a garment.

Not all fabrics need preshrinking. Many wools and silks are "needle-ready," and need nothing more than a touch-up with the iron before you lay out and cut the pattern pieces.

Press the preshrunk fabric before you cut out the pattern pieces and hang it on a hanger so it won't wrinkle. Press and hang your pattern pieces, too. They'll be easier to work with.

# Straightening the Grain

Even though fabric is woven straight (with the lengthwise and crosswise threads at right angles to each other), it is often pulled off-grain during the finishing process or as it is wound onto the bolt. If you cut and sew a garment off-grain, it may never hang the way you expect it to.

So, before you lay out your pattern pieces, check that the fabric is on the "straight of the grain," that is, with all edges, selvage, and cross grain straight and at right angles. Make a snip through the selvage about 1 in. to 2 in. from one of the raw edges. Tear the fabric if it tears easily and without distortion, or pull one thread out and cut along the area it was pulled from. (Some fabric stores will do this when you buy the fabric.)

Now fold the fabric in half, with selvages together. Press the fabric and place it on a flat surface. The selvage and cross grain should be straight and at right angles to each other; cross-grain threads should lie on top of one another.

If the fabric is off-grain, pull the fabric firmly from the corners along the bias to straighten it. If you have a lot of yardage, work down the length of the fabric, pulling every 12 in. from corner to corner. This task is easily accomplished with two people, but if you're working alone, you can press the fabric, stretching it along the bias as you work, as shown in the photo on the facing page.

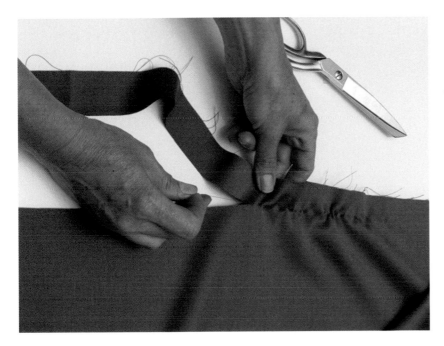

*To find the "straight of the grain," tear the fabric or pull a thread and cut along the crosswise grain. Check that the selvage and cross grain are straight and at right angles.*

# 3 Getting the Right Fit

Part of the fun of sewing for yourself is to get the best fit possible. Fitting is the process of adjusting or altering a commercial pattern so that it will exactly fit the person who will wear the garment. It is rare for anyone to have precisely the same measurements as a commercial pattern, and seldom can a pattern be used straight out of the envelope without changes. Altering and customizing the pattern are as much a part of creating clothes as sewing and pressing are.

Fitting has an undeserved reputation for being difficult. It's not, but it can be time-consuming—up to one-third of the time it takes to construct an entire garment is spent preparing and adjusting the pattern. Once you know how your body differs from the pattern, you can adjust all your patterns for your specific hip or waist measurements, preferred length, or other variations. With all the time you'll invest in perfecting a pattern, it certainly pays to have a collection of favorites that you can use again and again.

Because fitting is a trial-and-error process, it helps to take a fitting class or to have a friend who sews or a professional dressmaker assist you in measuring and basic fitting. Reference books help too.

One of the secrets to success in sewing is the process of "proofing" the pattern. When you proof a pattern, you make certain that the skirt will fit around your body and that it will be the right length. Once that's accomplished, pin the tissue pieces together and try on the pattern to check the style, details, and silhouette. When you have a pattern that's exactly customized to the shape of your body, you're ready to cut out the fabric and begin sewing a garment you can be sure you'll enjoy wearing.

Make it your goal to add pattern adjustment and fitting to your repertoire of sewing skills, expanding your knowledge bit by bit with each project.

# The Basics

*For many people, fitting is a mystery—but it needn't be.*
*There are four basic steps. Take them one at a time.*
*It also helps to have a few tools handy.*

# Four Basic Steps

If you follow these four simple steps before you cut your fabric, any fitting you do during construction will be fine-tuning, not a major overhaul.

**1**. Compare your body measurements to those of the flat pattern (pp. 28-29).

**2**. Proof the pattern to ensure that the skirt will be the right length and will fit around your body (pp. 30-33).

**3**. Pin the pattern pieces together as they will be sewn and try on the pattern (p. 40). Adjust for swayback (pp. 40-41), round tummy (p. 42) or large hips (p. 43).

**4**. Make any desired changes to the pattern for pockets (p. 34), walking ease (p. 35), linings (p. 36) or changes in grainline (pp. 37-39). Pin-fit again if necessary, and transfer any further adjustments to the pattern.

# Tools

Adjusting patterns is much simpler and the results are more professional if you use the right tools. Each tool has its own specific uses for the various patternmaking tasks; none substitutes for another. As you grow more familiar with them, they'll become like extensions of your hands.

Acquire the following, arranged here in order of necessity:

Of course, you'll need a measuring tape and 6-in. gauge.

A 2-in. by 18-in. C-Thru ruler is invaluable for creating straight lines, finding right angles, lengthening, shortening, and more.

A metal hip curve is just right for curving and shaping the hips, waist, and legs. (This professional patternmaker's tool is available at stores that sell patternmaking supplies or from mail-order sources.)

Once you use a metal yardstick you'll never again use a wooden one. It's great for making clean, long straight lines and edges.

There are several additional tools you'll find useful when adjusting your pattern—glue, tape, strips of elastic, tracing paper and pattern tissue, pencils and pens, chalk, Clo-chalk, dressmaker's pencils, right-angle ruler, full-length mirror, hand mirror, embroidery floss and chenille needle, scissors, and appliqué scissors. The list will continue to grow as you find your own way of working.

# Comparing Measurements

*The first step in altering your pattern is to compare your body measurements with the pattern's.*

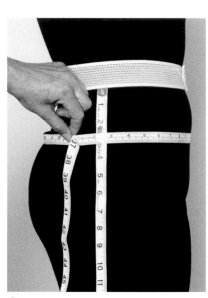

1 *Measure waistline.*

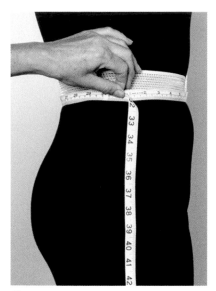

2 *Measure high hip or tummy.*

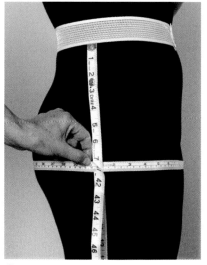

3 *Measure full hip, and from waist to full hip.*

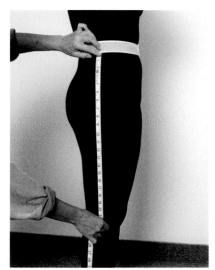

4 *Measure finished length.*

## Measure Your Body

The four critical measurements are the waist, high hip/tummy, full hip, and finished length. Make a note of these. They're essential for altering and fitting your pattern.

When measuring, wear the underclothing and shoes you might wear with the skirt.

**Waist:** Pin a length of wide elastic around your body where you'd like the skirt waistline to be. Measure over the elastic, holding a finger underneath the tape measure to allow an adequate amount of ease **(1)**.

**High hip/tummy:** Check your side view in a full-length mirror and measure your high hip/tummy wherever your figure is largest—between 1½ in. and 4 in. below the waist **(2)**. Be sure the tape measure doesn't rise up slightly at center front. Also measure from waist to high hip.

**Full hip:** Check your side view again and measure around your hips at their fullest point (this is the full-hip measurement). Also measure from your waist to your full hip **(3)**.

**Finished length:** Measure from the waistline at the side seam or front to the desired finished length **(4)**. (Or measure the length of your favorite skirt of similar style.)

# Measure Your Pattern

To make it easier to measure the pattern, take it out of the envelope and spread it out on a flat, uncluttered work table.

**Waist:** Hold the tape measure on its edge (to make it easier to follow the pattern's curves) and measure the waist along the stitching line, excluding seam allowances, tucks, pleats, or darts **(1)**. Pin these in position or simply skip over them when measuring—this will give you the actual measurements of the finished skirt. (Because of the ease built into the pattern, this measurement should be larger than the waist size listed on the pattern envelope.)

**High hip/tummy:** If you have a rounded tummy or high round hips, take an additional measurement 1½ to 4 in. below the waistline of your pattern.

**Full hip:** The full-hip measurement on the pattern will be the same distance from the waist as the measurement on your body. If your skirt has tucks or pleats, pin them into position first to get a true measurement of the finished garment **(2)**.

**Finished length:** Along the skirt's center front or side seamline, measure from the waistline to the bottom edge of the desired hem.

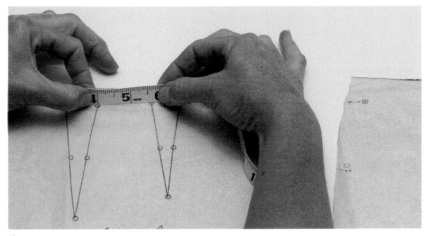

1 *Measure the waistline, excluding the darts, tucks, pleats, and seam allowances.*

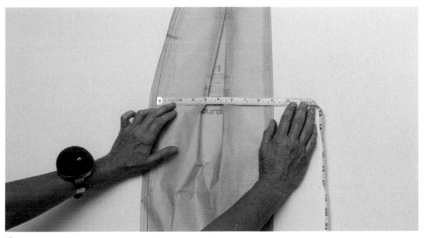

2 *Measure the pattern at full hip with the pleats pinned in position.*

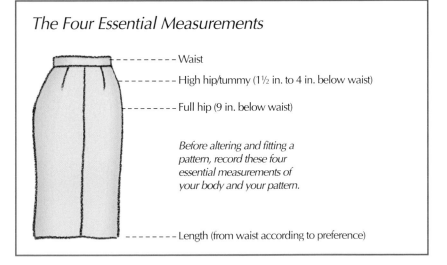

## The Four Essential Measurements

Waist

High hip/tummy (1½ in. to 4 in. below waist)

Full hip (9 in. below waist)

*Before altering and fitting a pattern, record these four essential measurements of your body and your pattern.*

Length (from waist according to preference)

# Proofing the Pattern

*Adjust the length and width of the flat pattern before you try it on to reduce the amount of fitting you'll need to do later.*

It's more efficient to lengthen or shorten your pattern before you add width so that you'll be working only with the necessary length. You'll also be able to blend the side seamlines easily and accurately as you smooth the jog that often occurs when you change the length of the garment.

If you need to lengthen or shorten your skirt 2 in. or less, simply add or subtract length at the hem. If you need to adjust it more than 2 in., alter the body of the skirt at the lengthen/shorten line.

If your pattern doesn't have a lengthen/shorten line, add one so you will be able to realign the top and bottom halves of the skirt. To do this, extend the grainline; then draw a line at a right angle to it at the point where you want to lengthen or shorten your skirt.

If your skirt is shaped at the hem, as in a gored, flared, or pegged skirt, or if it has a kick pleat, French vent, or hem detail, lengthen or shorten below the full hip so as not to interfere with the design detail.

You may need more fabric if you lengthen or widen the skirt significantly. To find out for sure, do a trial layout of your pattern pieces on paper or on a gridded cutting board.

## Lengthening a Pattern

Cut along the lengthen/shorten line and tape or glue a piece of tissue paper along one cut edge, overlapping the pattern and tissue edges about 1/2 in. (You can use scrap pattern tissue, as long as it's as wide as the pattern piece and at least 1 in. longer than the amount you're adding to the skirt.)

On the scrap tissue, parallel to the lengthen/shorten line, mark the amount you want to add to the skirt. Extend the grainline through the scrap tissue. Line it up with the grainline on the other half of the skirt pattern and glue or tape the scrap tissue in place.

If you're not also changing the width of the skirt, simply draw the side seamlines on the scrap tissue and blend the seamlines of the skirt halves.

If you are changing the skirt width, make these adjustments (p. 31) and blend all the seamlines in one operation.

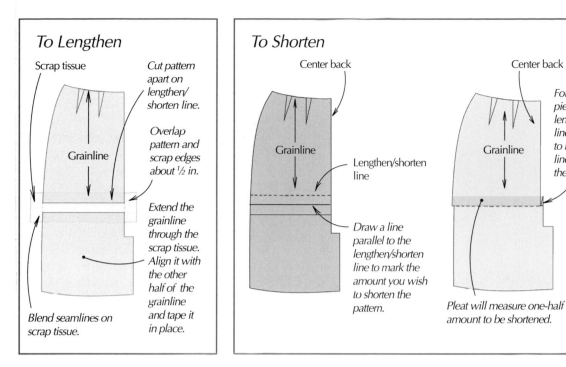

**To Lengthen**

Scrap tissue

Grainline

Cut pattern apart on lengthen/ shorten line.

Overlap pattern and scrap edges about ½ in.

Extend the grainline through the scrap tissue. Align it with the other half of the grainline and tape it in place.

Blend seamlines on scrap tissue.

**To Shorten**

Center back

Grainline

Lengthen/shorten line

Draw a line parallel to the lengthen/shorten line to mark the amount you wish to shorten the pattern.

Center back

Grainline

Fold the pattern piece along the lengthen/shorten line. Bring the fold to meet the drawn line. Tape or glue the fold in place.

Pleat will measure one-half amount to be shortened.

## Shortening a Pattern

Mark the amount you want to shorten your pattern by drawing a line parallel to the lengthen/shorten line.

Fold the pattern piece along the lenthen/shorten line and then lift the fold to meet the drawn line. Glue or tape the pattern piece in position. The pleat that forms should be half the total amount to be shortened (for example, if you're shortening the skirt 1½ in., the pleat will be ¾ in. wide).

Make width adjustments, if needed, at the hip or waist. Connect and blend the seamlines.

## Adjusting Width

Adjusting width is the most common pattern alteration, and it pays to master it from the start. Increase or decrease skirt width at the side seams only. If you add width at center front or back, the darts/tucks will be positioned too far apart.

Although you'll decrease width less frequently, the same principles apply for both increasing and decreasing. Adjust the side seams on the pattern tissue, drawing in new cutting lines. This will allow you to pin the tissue together along the stitching lines and try on the paper pattern to test the fit.

The total amount of adjusted width should be divided evenly among the quarters of the skirt—if an extra 2 in. is needed, for example, add ½ in. at each side seam.

# CALCULATING PATTERN EASE

Two types of ease are built into the pattern: wearing ease and design ease. Wearing ease is the amount of extra fabric you need to move comfortably in a garment. Design ease is the amount of extra fabric the designer or patternmaker adds to give the garment a certain style and look. The total amount of ease is the difference between the size measurements on the pattern envelope and the actual measurements of the pattern.

For example, the size chart on the pattern envelope or in the pattern book may indicate that a size 10 pattern has a waist of 26 in. and hips of 34 in. The skirt's flat pattern, however, measures 27½ in. at the waist and 38 in. at the hip. This means there is 1½ in. of ease in the waist and 4 in. in the hip, which is standard for a straight skirt.

*Flat-pattern measurement – Envelope measurement = Amount of ease*

To determine the amount of ease in your pattern, measure the flat pattern (p. 29) and compare these figures to the body measurements on the pattern envelope. Write down the amount of ease your pattern allows in the waist, high hip, and full hip. When you adjust your pattern for your body measurements, you want to maintain this amount of pattern ease (as shown in the chart below).

You can add a total of up to 8 in. (2 in. at each side seam) to the waist and/or hip before the shape becomes distorted. If you need to add more width than this, you should use a larger-size pattern.

It's also possible to make varying adjustments to the hip, high hip, and waist. Figures with a rounded tummy or high round hip, for example, may need extra width at the waist as well as at the high hip to achieve a smooth line (pp. 42-43). This is especially true for small-waisted figures (an elasticized fitted waistband, p. 96, works very well on these shapes).

After you've made all necessary adjustments, use 1-in. side seams to build in extra fitting insurance. This will allow you enough extra fabric to alter the skirt while you're

## CALCULATING THE WIDTH ADJUSTMENT

Make a copy of this chart and record your body measurements, the flat-pattern's measurements, and the pattern ease. The chart will help you determine how much to adjust your pattern at each seam for the best fit, while retaining the right amount of wearing and design ease.

| | Waist | High hip/ tummy | Full hip |
|---|---|---|---|
| Body Measurement | 29 | | |
| Plus Ease (as calculated above) | 1½ | | |
| Total | 30½ | | |
| Minus Flat-Pattern Measurement | 27½ | | |
| Adjustment to Pattern (distributed evenly at side-seam allowances) | 3 | | |

sewing; the extra seam width can always be trimmed or evened afterward.

Make dots on the tissue with a pencil to mark the amount you need to adjust the side seams at waist, high hip, and full hip. If needed, attach scrap tissue paper to the side seams to add enough width **(1)**. Make sure you maintain the hip ease at your full-hip measurement.

Use a hip curve to connect the dots, adding the same amount you added to the full hip all the way down the seam to the hem, in order to retain the original silhouette of the skirt.

Remember to adjust the waistband pattern piece if you make any changes in the skirt width at the waistline. If you add ½ in. to each of the skirt's side seams, for example, you'll also need to add 2 in. to the waistband by adding 1 in. to each waistband side seam.

As you become more adept at making and fitting skirts, you may prefer simply to chalk-mark the amount that you need to add or subtract directly onto the fabric **(2)**, and cut.

A hip curve will help you redraw the new silhouette of the skirt perfectly.

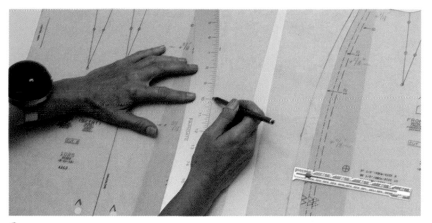

1 Add extra width to the side seams of the pattern pieces with tissue paper.

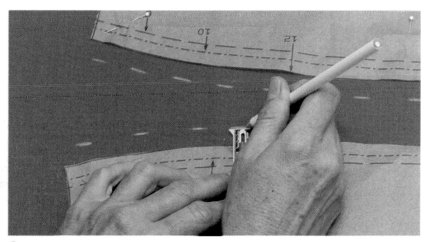

2 Mark additions directly onto fabric.

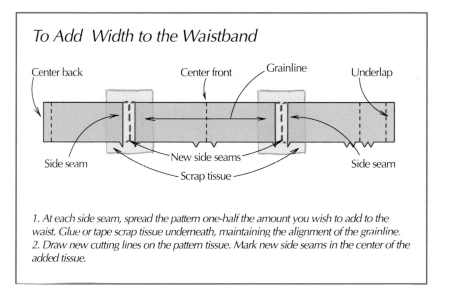

## To Add Width to the Waistband

Center back   Center front   Grainline   Underlap

Side seam   New side seams   Side seam

Scrap tissue

1. At each side seam, spread the pattern one-half the amount you wish to add to the waist. Glue or tape scrap tissue underneath, maintaining the alignment of the grainline.
2. Draw new cutting lines on the pattern tissue. Mark new side seams in the center of the added tissue.

# Customizing the Pattern

*A few simple, optional alterations to the flat pattern might make your garment more attractive and comfortable. Consider pockets, linings, and additional walking ease.*

## Adding a Pocket

If your pattern does not have a pocket, borrow one from another pattern. When you find a pocket that works well, copy it and save it for future use.

Position the pocket pattern so it extends into the waistband and mark the opening. If necessary, shape the side seam so it is the same as the side seam on your skirt. (Some skirts are curved to the shape of the hip, others are straight.) Position the pocket pattern on the skirt pattern, aligning them at the waistline, and trace the skirt's side seam onto the pocket.

Transfer the markings for the pocket opening with tiny snips or chalk marks on the wrong side of the fabric.

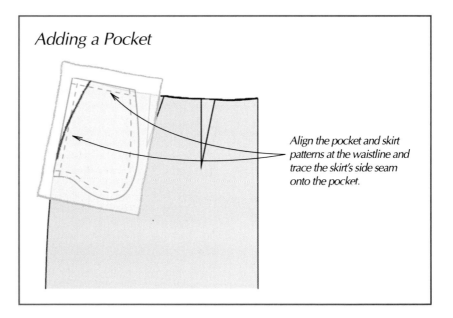

*Adding a Pocket*

Align the pocket and skirt patterns at the waistline and trace the skirt's side seam onto the pocket.

# Adding Walking Ease

Walking ease, a secret of fine dressmakers and never calculated in commercial patterns, is a simple alteration that makes kick pleats, French vents, slits, front openings, button-front and wrap skirts hang perfectly straight. In fact, the straightness is an optical illusion.

When a garment is cut straight, there's a natural tendency for it to hang open at the hem. If you add walking ease, however, skirts appear to hang arrow-straight.

When you add walking ease, you do not change the original grainline of the garment. Make this pattern change after all other adjustments are completed.

The amount of ease is based on the length of the garment and weight of the fabric.

**Kick Pleats, French Vents, Slits** Add walking ease at the front or back seamline, depending on the placement of the kick pleat, French vent, or slit. Add ½ in. for a knee-length (19-in. to 24-in.) skirt, 1 in. for a mid-calf (32-in. to 36-in.) skirt. Add slightly more (⅛ in. to ¼ in.) for heavy or thick fabrics. Adjust the lining pattern too (p. 36).

On the skirt-pattern piece, cut along the seamline/vent fold line from the hem to the waist. Tape or glue a scrap of tissue along one edge. Position the other edge so that the walking ease is added at the bottom of the hem and tapers to nothing at the waist end of the seam.

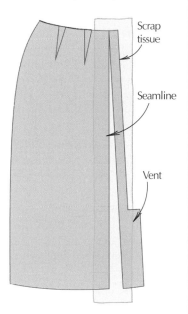

### Adding Walking Ease to a Pleat, Vent, or Slit

Scrap tissue

Seamline

Vent

*1. Cut along the seamline/vent fold line from the hem to the waist.*
*2. Add walking ease at the bottom of the hem by spreading the pattern and adding scrap tissue. Taper the slit in the pattern to nothing at the waistline.*

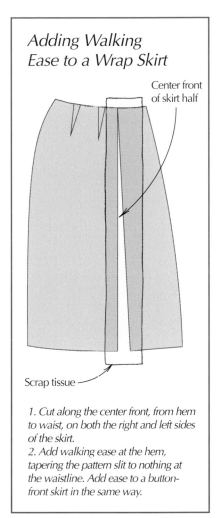

### Adding Walking Ease to a Wrap Skirt

Center front of skirt half

Scrap tissue

*1. Cut along the center front, from hem to waist, on both the right and left sides of the skirt.*
*2. Add walking ease at the hem, tapering the pattern slit to nothing at the waistline. Add ease to a button-front skirt in the same way.*

**Other Skirt Styles** For wrap or button-front styles, add ½ in. of ease for knee-length skirts, 1 in. for mid-calf-length skirts. Add the walking ease at the center front, from hem to waist, on both the left and the right sides of the skirt.

If your fabric is a plaid or stripe, or if it has a strong vertical design, add walking ease at the side seams.

For skirts with side buttons, add walking ease at the front and back side seams.

# Adding a Lining

Lining a skirt has multiple benefits: It gives a finished look to the inside of your garment, makes the skirt easy to slide on and off, and helps it stay wrinkle-free. In addition, a lining keeps the skirt fabric from clinging and makes a lightweight fabric opaque.

Even if the skirt pattern includes a lining, I prefer to cut one from the skirt pattern pieces. (For a list of suggested lining fabrics, see p. 21.) Lining fabrics are firmly woven and usually have much less give than the skirt fabric, so don't make the lining smaller than the skirt.

Cutting and constructing a lining is simple and fast. Linings for skirts with special details such as a French vent, however, may require additional adjustments, as shown in the drawing below. When you sew, stitch the lining's side seams slightly narrower ($\frac{1}{8}$ in.) to allow for sitting room and to keep the seams from pulling out.

Cut the lining so the hem will be at least 1 in. shorter than the skirt, while covering the raw edge of the skirt hem. Different lining-hem finishes may require that you cut the lining to slightly different lengths (pp. 84-85). If you're not sure how you're going to finish the lining hem, simply cut the lining 1 in. shorter than your skirt. Trim as needed.

## LINING A SKIRT WITH A FRENCH VENT

1. To adjust the skirt pattern to be used for the lining, fold the pattern piece back along the seamline and vent fold line. Trace the cut edge of the vent onto the pattern.

2. Add seam allowances by drawing a new cutting line $1\frac{1}{4}$ in. from the traced line, as shown in the drawing. This allows for the skirt's $\frac{5}{8}$-in. seam allowance plus the lining's $\frac{5}{8}$-in. seam allowance. The skirt and the finished lining will be flush at the vent opening.

3. Now draw the $\frac{5}{8}$-in. seam allowance of the lining vent, including the corner, as shown. Don't skip this step. You'll be reinforcing the seamlines at the corner, so you'll want them to be clearly marked.

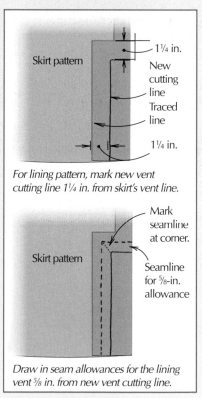

*For lining pattern, mark new vent cutting line $1\frac{1}{4}$ in. from skirt's vent line.*

*Draw in seam allowances for the lining vent $\frac{5}{8}$ in. from new vent cutting line.*

# Changing the Grainline of a Flared Skirt

The drape and flattering effect of an A-line or gored flared skirt can be changed significantly by repositioning the grainline on the pattern pieces.

Lengthwise grain is often placed at center front and center back of the pattern, on the lengthwise fold, which makes the front and back one pattern piece. This layout is common on commercial patterns because less fabric is required than with other layouts. It's the least flattering, however, as it results in a wide silhouette that broadens any figure and exaggerates a tummy. In addition, the bias at the side seam may stretch, creating an uneven hem.

Two alternate lengthwise-grain positions and one bias-grain position for the same skirt panels are shown on p. 38. Treat both front and back pattern pieces in the same way. Remember that you may need additional fabric if you change the grainline. To figure out the yardage you'll need, do a trial layout on paper that is the width of your fabric or on a gridded cutting board. You can reposition the grainline for any type of fabric.

### Lengthwise Grain in Center of Front and Back Panels

Often used by Ralph Lauren, this cut is very flattering and slimming, especially for the pear-shaped figure. Because the fullness hangs evenly around the skirt, an uneven hem is less likely. This layout is a perfect choice for rayons, knits, or other fabrics that may stretch at the hem.

To alter the pattern, simply fold the skirt panel in half, center seam to side seam. The waist shape will not match, but that's okay. Draw in a new grainline down the center of each panel. (Add seam allowances at center front and back if the original pattern was one piece cut on the fold.)

### Lengthwise Grain Parallel to Side Seam

If the straight of the grain is parallel to the side seam, the skirt's fullness hangs at the center. The center seam is on the bias and may tend to stretch. This styling creates a strong vertical line, which is especially effective with striped fabrics.

This layout broadens the figure and emphasizes a protruding tummy or derriere, but is a good choice for a figure with roundness at the side of the hips—the straight of the grain flattens out the curve.

### Bias Grain

The 45° diagonal line through the lengthwise and crosswise grain of the fabric is the bias. A bias-cut skirt requires more fabric than any of the other layouts, but nothing else has such a beautiful, flowing drape.

The bias cut will reveal curves and bulges, however, and garment construction and hemming take a bit of special care. If you are adapting a pattern with a one-piece front or back to a bias layout, add seam allowances to the center front and back. This way, the garment will hang without twisting to one side.

# Different Grainlines — Different Effects

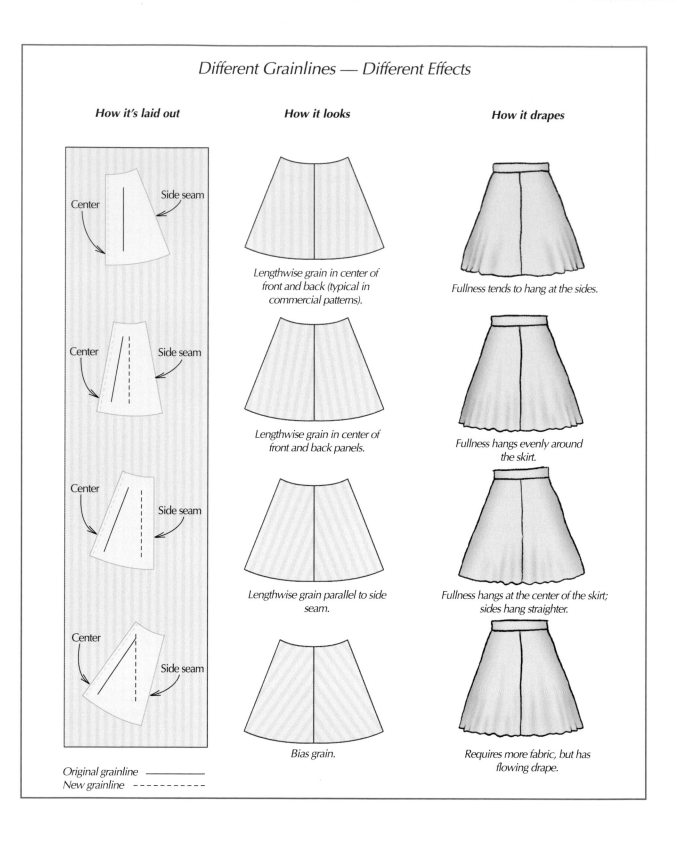

**How it's laid out**

**How it looks**

**How it drapes**

Center / Side seam

Lengthwise grain in center of front and back (typical in commercial patterns).

Fullness tends to hang at the sides.

Center / Side seam

Lengthwise grain in center of front and back panels.

Fullness hangs evenly around the skirt.

Center / Side seam

Lengthwise grain parallel to side seam.

Fullness hangs at the center of the skirt; sides hang straighter.

Center / Side seam

Bias grain.

Requires more fabric, but has flowing drape.

Original grainline  ——————
New grainline  - - - - - - - - -

The simplest way to alter a pattern for the bias cut is to use a right-angle ruler that has a 45° angle marked on it. An alternative is to mark lengthwise and crosswise grains with a C-Thru ruler. Then fold the fabric at a right angle through the intersection of the grainlines so the lines are superimposed on each other. Draw a line along the fold to mark the bias grainline. Mark a second bias grainline at 90° to the first. This way, when you turn over the pattern piece to cut out the second half, you can easily position it.

Place bias-cut pattern pieces on a single layer of fabric, keeping the pattern in a one-way layout, that is, with the nap of the fabric always in one direction. All the hems will be facing the same way.

When cutting two front or back pieces in one layer of cloth, be sure to flip the pattern piece over to cut the second half so that they will be mirror images.

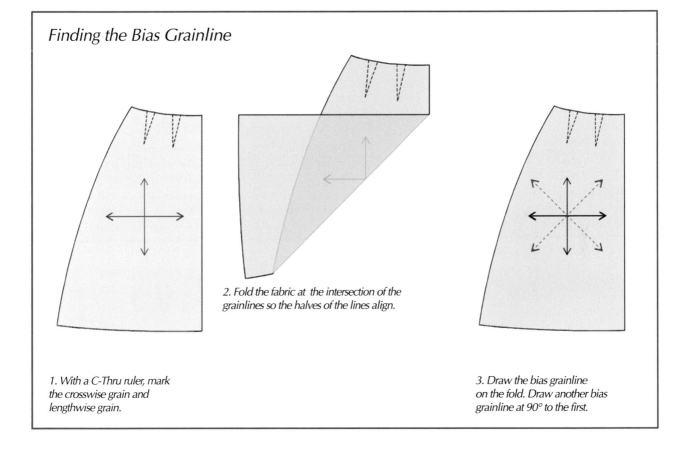

*Finding the Bias Grainline*

*1. With a C-Thru ruler, mark the crosswise grain and lengthwise grain.*

*2. Fold the fabric at the intersection of the grainlines so the halves of the lines align.*

*3. Draw the bias grainline on the fold. Draw another bias grainline at 90° to the first.*

# Pin-Fitting Adjustments

*There's no substitute for pin-fitting your pattern and altering it as carefully as you can before you cut the fabric.*

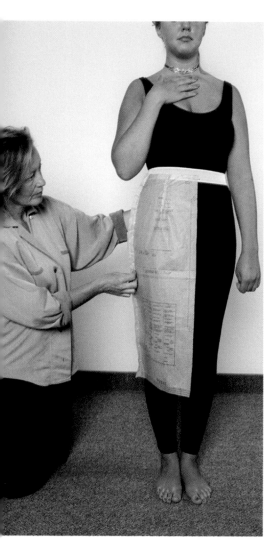

Once the two-dimensional flat pattern has been adjusted, it's time to have a look at your pattern in three dimensions.

Pin-fitting the pattern on your body, just as if it were the finished skirt, allows you to adjust for aspects of your body profile that are not accounted for by measurements alone. A swayback, a protruding tummy, and a fuller than average derrière, for example, may prevent your skirt pattern from fitting well. These very common adjustments are best made on the pattern tissue, now, before you cut out the garment.

## Try on the Pattern

Pin the pattern together and try it on as if it were the finished skirt. Place pins parallel to the stitching lines along the seams. Pin any darts, tucks, or pleats in position.

Hold the pattern in place at the waistline with a 1-in.-wide length of elastic. Position the center fronts and backs and check the fit, length, and overall styling in a full-length mirror. It takes only a bit of practice to develop an eye for the way the finished garment will look.

Use a large hand mirror to see the back view. A knowledgeable friend is also a great help!

After you check the fit and length, and have made the necessary adjustments, see if the skirt needs an adjustment for swayback or a protruding tummy.

## Adjusting for Swayback

If the skirt needs some adjustment for swayback, you'll find horizontal wrinkles at the center back of the pin-fitted skirt pattern, just below the waistband. Here's how to estimate the amount you'll need to remove at center back for the skirt to lie smoothly.

While pin-fitting, lower the waistline at center back by slipping the pattern slightly under the elastic until the wrinkles are eliminated. Mark the pattern tissue with a pen or pencil right under the elastic at center back. The amount you'll need to remove usually ranges from 1/4 in. to 1 1/2 in.

Pin all darts, pleats, or tucks in place. Then draw a new line to eliminate the desired amount of pattern tissue, starting at center back and gradually meeting the waistline at the side seams. The hip curve is the perfect tool for drawing this new waistline. If your skirt has gathers, the line is less critical, so simply draw, freehand, an even, slightly curved line from center back to side seam.

Overlap the pattern pieces for the amount of the adjustment at the center-back seamline, tapering to nothing at the side seams. Redraw the lines for darts, tucks, and the center-back seam. Make corresponding adjustments to the back facing. Avoid the pins and cut along the redrawn waistline.

If you're working without a partner, it may be difficult to determine the exact amount you'll need to remove. That's okay. Estimate now and fine-tune the fit later while you're constructing the garment. You can make this swayback alteration just before you apply the waistband to the skirt, but you may need to shorten the zipper, too. It's easiest to make pattern adjustments before cutting, then double-check them during the garment's construction.

If your skirt has a raised waistband (p. 101), make the swayback adjustment by cutting the pattern back along the waistline, from the center back to ⅛ in. from the side seam.

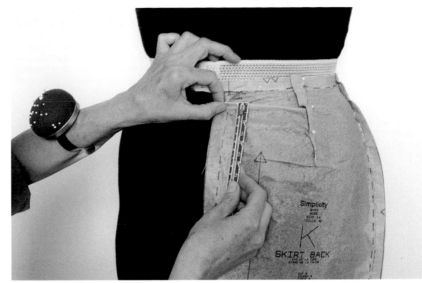

*To adjust for swayback, lower the waistline at center back until the horizontal wrinkles are eliminated. You may need to remove from ¼ in. to 1½ in. of excess pattern tissue.*

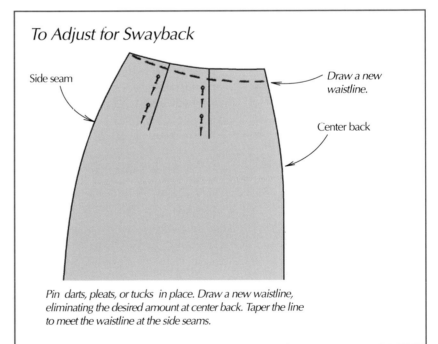

## To Adjust for Swayback

Side seam

Draw a new waistline.

Center back

*Pin darts, pleats, or tucks in place. Draw a new waistline, eliminating the desired amount at center back. Taper the line to meet the waistline at the side seams.*

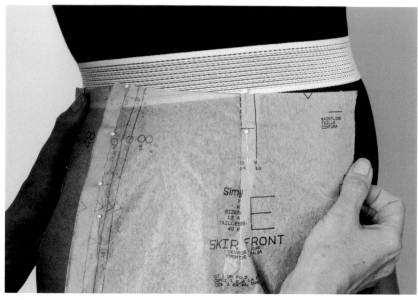

*If the pattern piece you're pin-fitting sits below the waistline because of a protruding tummy, you need to add extra length at center front.*

# Adjusting for a Round Tummy

To adjust for a round tummy, you usually need to add not only extra width to your pattern (pp. 31-33), but also extra length at center front. When pin-fitting, check that the skirt pattern sits correctly at the waistline. If it doesn't, you'll need to correct it by adding length to the pattern with scrap tissue. This little adjustment can actually minimize the curve visually.

Add enough length so that the pattern meets the waistline correctly and hangs over the tummy smoothly. Exactly how much to add is hard to estimate, but it's best to allow a little extra. Average amounts range from $\frac{3}{8}$ in. (which doesn't sound like much, but can make a small tummy nearly vanish) to about $2\frac{1}{2}$ in.

Before you begin, pin any pleats, tucks, and darts in place. Draw a line on the scrap tissue to indicate the additional pattern length at center front and taper to nothing at the side seams. Curve the cutting line slightly outward over the tummy using the hip curve. Trim the tissue with the pleats, tucks, and darts in position.

A figure with a round tummy rarely is flattered by a darted-front skirt. Eliminate the darts and ease the entire amount across the front using the technique known as staystitch plus (p. 60).

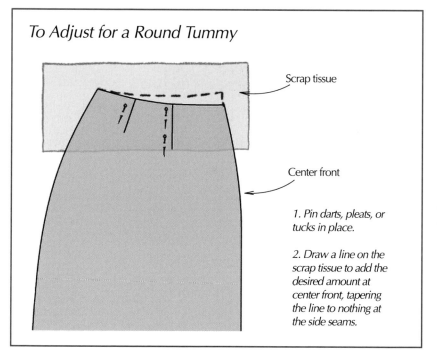

## To Adjust for a Round Tummy

Scrap tissue

Center front

*1. Pin darts, pleats, or tucks in place.*

*2. Draw a line on the scrap tissue to add the desired amount at center front, tapering the line to nothing at the side seams.*

# Adjusting for Full-Hip Measurements

The straight darts on a pattern are designed for an "average" full-hip measurement, but you can curve the back darts to the exact shape of your figure. The darts should point toward and end 1 in. to 1½ in. away from the fullest part of the figure. Shorten or lengthen them as needed.

Working from the midpoint of the dart, add or subtract ⅛ in. from each of the original dart lines. Use the hip curve to re-mark the stitching line, beginning and ending at the top and bottom of the dart.

For rounded full hips, scoop in the legs of the darts, allowing ¼ in. of extra fabric in the garment per dart.

For flat or low derrières and narrow full hips, curve the darts out, eliminating ¼ in. of fabric from the garment per dart.

Mark the position of the new end of the dart, and redraw the legs to reconnect them to their original positions at the waist.

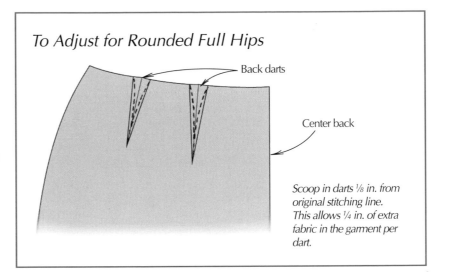

*To Adjust for Rounded Full Hips*

Back darts

Center back

*Scoop in darts ⅛ in. from original stitching line. This allows ¼ in. of extra fabric in the garment per dart.*

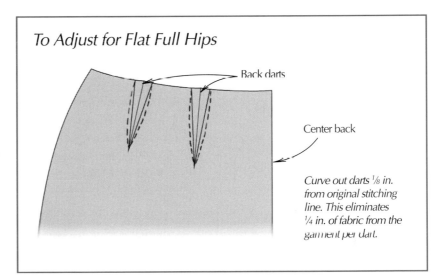

*To Adjust for Flat Full Hips*

Back darts

Center back

*Curve out darts ⅛ in. from original stitching line. This eliminates ¼ in. of fabric from the garment per dart.*

# 4 Construction Guidelines

Once you've made all your pattern adjustments, you're probably eager to start sewing. But before you begin, take some time to think through the sewing sequence and plan for any style modifications, details, and finishes you've chosen. Just as an architect needs to understand the whole process of constructing a building, a sewer needs to understand the progression of steps in a garment's construction and how each step leads to the next.

The pattern instruction sheet is your starting point. Read the instructions through and think about the construction sequence. Decide which techniques you want to use and which ones you want to change or modify. For example, you may decide to try a waistband style different from the one provided in the pattern or to change the way you put in the zipper. Also think about topstitching details, seam finishes, and the hem width and finish. If you decide to make any changes in construction techniques or the sewing sequence, write notes to yourself right on the pattern instruction sheet. For easy reference, also note the pages of this book where the techniques you'd like to try are explained in detail.

Before you begin to work on the garment, experiment with scraps of your skirt and lining fabrics. Make sample seams and try different seam and hem finishes. With the thread and needle size recommended for your fabric, test for the best stitch length. Press these samples to determine the best heat setting for your iron. If you're planning to use a fusible interfacing, fuse a scrap of it to your fabric to test their compatibility. Be sure to try any new or difficult technique you'd like to use on your garment ahead of time, and save all your samples for future reference.

# Construction Chronology

*This sequence illustrates the construction steps for a straight or flared skirt with darts or tucks, pockets in the side seam, a center back zipper, and a lining. It is intended as a guide for developing your own order of construction for sewing your skirt. Following a "generic" sequence such as this is helpful when you add features (a lining, for instance) to a pattern that doesn't have them.*

## Steps in Making a Skirt

Before you begin, read the guidesheet and mark up all pattern, cutting, and construction changes.

**1.** Adjust the pattern for fit and design.

**2.** Cut out all the pattern pieces. Transfer markings to fabric.

**3.** Apply interfacing, as needed, at pocket, waistband, or zipper openings.

**4.** Staystitch interfacing.

**5.** Overlock edges if using serger to finish seams. Apply pockets while serging the side seams.

**6.** Stitch darts or tucks. Apply pockets.

**7.** Stitch center-back seam, forming French vent if there is one. Insert zipper.

**8.** Pin side seams, wrong sides together, vertically along the seamlines. Try on, altering as needed. Stitch side seams. Press. Try on again, fine-tuning for swayback, tummy, and waistline measurements.

**9.** Construct lining: Stitch center back seam, allowing room for zipper and vent opening. Stitch side seams.

**10.** Insert lining. Machine baste at waist, forming tucks at darts. Handsew around zipper.

**11.** Apply waistband.

**12.** Apply closures.

**13.** Hem: Mark, press, trim, pin, and try on. Finish edge, stitch. Press.

**14.** Hem lining, attach at vent.

**15.** Final pressing to finish your skirt.

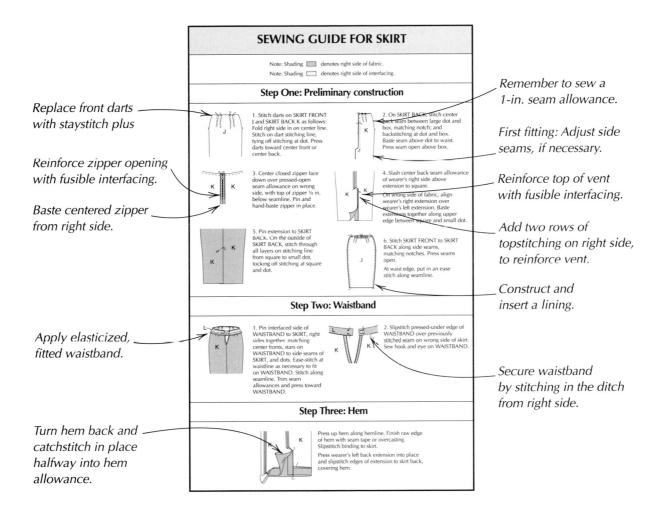

## SEWING GUIDE FOR SKIRT

Note: Shading ▢ denotes right side of fabric.
Note: Shading ▢ denotes right side of interfacing.

### Step One: Preliminary construction

**Replace front darts with staystitch plus**

1. Stitch darts on SKIRT FRONT J and SKIRT BACK K as follows: Fold right side in on center line. Stitch on dart stitching line, tying off stitching at dot. Press darts toward center front or center back.

2. On SKIRT BACK, stitch center back seam between large dot and box, matching notch; and backstitching at dot and box. Baste seam above dot to waist. Press seam open above box.

**Reinforce zipper opening with fusible interfacing.**

**Baste centered zipper from right side.**

3. Center closed zipper face down over pressed-open seam allowance on wrong side, with top of zipper ⅛ in. below seamline. Pin and hand-baste zipper in place.

4. Slash center back seam allowance of wearer's right side above extension to square.

On wrong side of fabric, align wearer's right extension over wearer's left extension. Baste extensions together along upper edge between square and small dot.

5. Pin extension to SKIRT BACK. On the outside of SKIRT BACK, stitch through all layers on stitching line from square to small dot, locking off stitching at square and dot.

6. Stitch SKIRT FRONT to SKIRT BACK along side seams, matching notches. Press seams open.

At waist edge, put in an ease stitch along seamline.

### Step Two: Waistband

**Apply elasticized, fitted waistband.**

1. Pin interfaced side of WAISTBAND to SKIRT, right sides together, matching center fronts, stars on WAISTBAND to side seams of SKIRT, and dots. Ease-stitch at waistline as necessary to fit on WAISTBAND. Stitch along seamline. Trim seam allowances and press toward WAISTBAND.

2. Slipstitch pressed-under edge of WAISTBAND over previously stitched seam on wrong side of skirt. Sew hook and eye on WAISTBAND.

### Step Three: Hem

**Turn hem back and catchstitch in place halfway into hem allowance.**

Press up hem along hemline. Finish raw edge of hem with seam tape or overcasting. Slipstitch binding to skirt.

Press wearer's left back extension into place and slipstitch edges of extension to skirt back, covering hem.

*Remember to sew a 1-in. seam allowance.*

*First fitting: Adjust side seams, if necessary.*

*Reinforce top of vent with fusible interfacing.*

*Add two rows of topstitching on right side, to reinforce vent.*

*Construct and insert a lining.*

*Secure waistband by stitching in the ditch from right side.*

Make sure you understand the instructions on your guidesheet. Remember it's just a beginning. There are many ways to enhance your pattern to get the fit and look you want. Mark your guidesheets with additional steps, reminders for fitting, and techniques to replace the pattern's suggestions.

# Cutting and Marking

*Now you're ready to cut out the pattern pieces and transfer the markings to the fabric. Don't rush this step.*

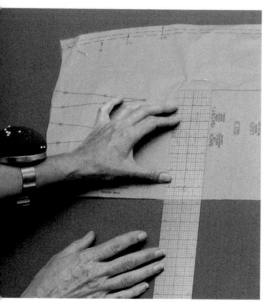

1 *Check that the grainline and selvage are parallel and the pattern pieces are on the grain.*

2 *Mark notches, darts, tucks, and centers with ¼-in. scissors snips.*

Take time and care when cutting and marking. An error of ¼ in. might not seem like much on a pattern piece, but as you cut and mark, your ¼ in. could quickly become an inch.

## Cutting

You'll save time and make fewer mistakes if you cut everything at one time, including the lining and interfacing.

Be precise and fastidious about placing the pattern pieces on the straight of the grain. Use a ruler to check that the grainline and selvage of the fabric are parallel to each other **(1).**

Sharp scissors are fine, but a rotary cutter and a mat will save you some time. Consider using weights, instead of pins, to hold your pattern in place.

## Marking

Mark notches, centers, darts, tucks, etc., with ¼-in. scissors snips whenever possible. They're easy to find, fast to make, and permanent **(2).** Use the tip of your scissors, not the rotary cutter—it's very easy to cut too deep.

Chalk, tracing paper, and pencils are all designed to mark the wrong side of the fabric. Don't use them on the right side of your garment. (An exception to this rule is Clo-chalk, a white powdery chalk that disappears within 24 hours or as soon as your garment is pressed or laundered.)

You can also use simple tailor's tacks to transfer markings from the pattern to your fabric. These tacks are easily identifiable from either side of the fabric and suitable for any type of marking. They work especially well for positioning darts, pleats, and tucks.

# MAKING TAILOR'S TACKS

Multistrand embroidery floss works well for making tailor's tacks because it's thick and won't pull out readily. I also use a chenille needle, which is sharp and has a large, easy-to-thread eye.

Make one small stitch through both layers of fabric on each pattern mark, leaving at least ½-in. tails at each end (**1**). Slowly peel the pattern tissue from the tacks without tearing it. Carefully pull open the fabric layers so that there is enough thread between them to clip the tacks and leave tails (**2**). These tacks on the inside (right side) of the cloth will be more uniform lengths, so you will be able to tell the right side of the fabric from the wrong side at a glance.

To mark any pleats or tucks, try using two different colors of embroidery floss to mark each set. Later, you'll be able to match the sets easily. (See p. 61.)

To mark a dart, make snip marks to mark the tops of the legs. Use tailor's tacks to mark the midpoints and tip of the dart. Then sculpt the dart by connecting the tacks with a hip curve and a fine-line chalk marker (**3**), and you'll have an easy-to-follow stitching guide.

Don't machine-stitch over tailor's tacks; they can get caught in the stitches and be tricky to pull out. Instead, baste or mark the area carefully, remove the tacks, then stitch by machine.

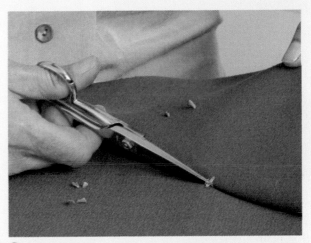

**2** *Pull the fabric apart and clip the tacks.*

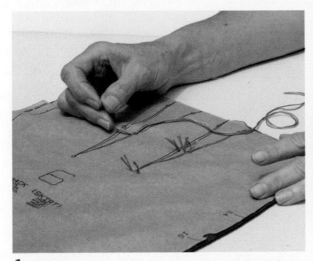

**1** *Mark darts with tailor's tacks, leaving ½-in. tails.*

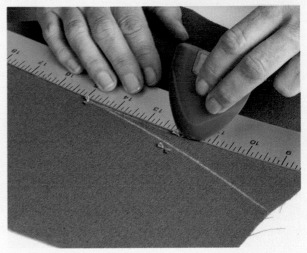

**3** *Use chalk and a hip curve to mark dart lines on the wrong side of the fabric.*

# Pressing

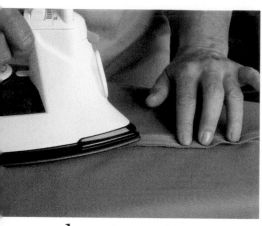

**1** *Press the seam flat on the wrong side, holding the seam halves open as you work.*

**2** *Press again from the right side, using a press cloth if necessary.*

*Pressing seams and darts is the secret to making clothes that look professional.*

## Tools

The best iron gets hot and stays hot and gives off a good shot of steam. Always test a scrap of your fabric to determine the best setting to use.

You'll also need a clapper/pointer, a hardwood tool for flattening seams and pressing points; a pressing ham, a contoured device that looks like its namesake and is used to shape darts and curved seams; and a press cloth.

Press cloths protect the surface of the garment fabric, and professionals rely on them. Use a cotton, see-through press cloth for cottons, silks, and linens; a specially treated, heavy drill (cotton twill) press cloth and a scrap of wool for pressing wools. The heavy cotton protects the wool fabric, particularly if you are ironing the right side of the fabric, and allows you to press with the iron set at a high temperature. Wool pressed against wool prevents the fabric from flattening and becoming shiny. (Professional tailors often sew a square of wool to one area of the heavy-cotton press cloth in order to have both at hand.)

Test your fabric to see if it can be pressed on the right side. If right-side pressing changes the appearance of the fabric, always use a press cloth. Your fingers are also important pressing tools, especially for fabrics that are slippery or don't hold shape easily. Finger-press all seams before using the iron.

## Techniques

After sewing each seam and dart, press it flat, as it was sewn, to blend the stitches, smooth the fabric, and erase puckers.

Then press the seams open on the wrong side of the fabric. Use your fingers and the point of the iron to open the seam halves to lie flat as you work **(1)**. Press the seam or dart again on the right side of the fabric, using the press cloth if necessary **(2)**.

Unlike ironing, which is a sliding motion, pressing is a lifting and lowering motion.

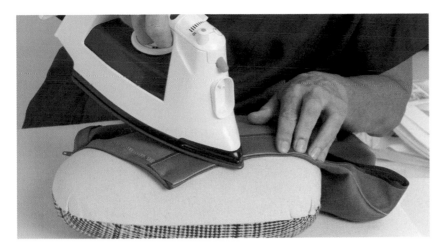

**3** *Shape curved darts and seams by pressing them over a ham.*

As you work, use the clapper to flatten and cool the pressed area. The hardwood absorbs heat and moisture, and the weight of the tool and the pounding flattens the stitched seam or dart. For some fabrics, such as cottons, rayons, and silks, just the weight of the clapper is enough to do the job; for wools, you may need to apply extra pressure.

Also press back darts and curved seams over the ham to build curves and shape the garment **(3)**. Press front darts over the ham's flattest part to avoid rounding them. Press all vertical darts toward the center of the garment.

After pressing, seams and darts should be so flat they almost disappear. Let the pressed area cool before readjusting the fabric on the ironing board.

## PRESSING THE STRETCH OUT OF BIAS

Before handling any piece of fabric that's been cut on the bias, press the stretch out. This technique is straight from the workrooms of French couture. After pressing, the seams of bias-cut skirt panels can be sewn with minimum distortion. After the garment is finished, the hem will not sag, and the skirt will be less likely to stretch in length and decrease in width.

Position the bias-cut skirt panel on a pressing surface that is long enough for the entire length. Steam-press, and as you do, gently stretch the fabric in the lengthwise direction of the skirt. Begin at one seam and work in radiating parallel lines across the panel to the other seam. Allow the fabric to cool before repositioning it. Repeat the process with all of the skirt panels. The hem may become uneven, but after you've measured it and hemmed it evenly, it will stay even.

*Steam-press while gently stretching the fabric lengthwise to ensure that the finished garment will hold its shape.*

# Seams and Seam Finishes

*Stitching seams is one of the basic components of sewing. With a little practice, you'll be able to sew perfect straight or curved seams and a variety of professional finishes.*

A Hong Kong seam finish, made with China silk, rayon, or silk bias strips, is a flat and elegant binding for hems and waistbands.

Before you begin sewing, always test for the best stitch length, needle size, and type of thread for your fabric. Test the stitch length for appearance and strength as well as for ease in ripping. A too-long stitch length uses less thread, but creates a puckered seam.

Keep a supply of different needles on hand and use only the best quality—this is not a place to skimp. Change the needle before you begin each new garment and any time the needle hits a pin (listen for the sound of a blunt or bent needle piercing the cloth).

If you notice skipped stitches, or if the thread keeps breaking or fraying, try a different-size needle. If that doesn't help, try another brand of needle.

# Sewing Perfect Seams

For smooth seams, always cut, stitch, and press seams in the same direction. For skirts, this usually means working along the length of the garment, from hem to waistline.

To sew long side seams, place pins vertically on the stitching line, positioned so that you can pull them out as you sew. This saves time and—because you're not sewing over pins—it also saves wear and tear on the machine.

Pin the top and bottom of the seam first. Next match the notches, then match or ease the fabric in between. A fabric with "tooth" grabs or sticks to itself and thus requires fewer pins than a slippery fabric that moves and slides. You may need to hand-baste some hard-to-handle fabrics, such as velvet, before stitching.

Most seams are sewn with right sides together, using a $5/8$-in. seam allowance. Some machines have this $5/8$-in. width marked on the throat plate. A magnetic seam guide, which acts as a "fence" along which you can guide the fabric, is also a very helpful tool (see photo 3 on p. 65).

Always press a seam after stitching and before crossing it with another seam or detail.

Remember, stitching and pressing go hand in hand.

## RIPPING OUT SEAMS

Ripping out seams is an essential part of sewing. Use the narrow point of the seam ripper to break a few stitches on one side of the seam. This frees the thread on the other side so that it can be pulled. Working from one end of the seam to the other, rip just a few stitches, grasp the thread with your fingers, and give it a good pull, disposing of the loose threads as you go.

Another way to rip stitches is to use the point of the ripper to break threads on one side of the fabric every $1/2$ in. to 1 in. along the seam and then pull the long freed-up thread on the other side. (The disadvantage is that on the first side you're left with broken threads all along the seam that need to be removed.)

Never work the curved portion of the seam ripper between the two layers of the seam unless the fabric is heavy and very firmly woven. Otherwise, you're liable to rip the fabric as well as the threads.

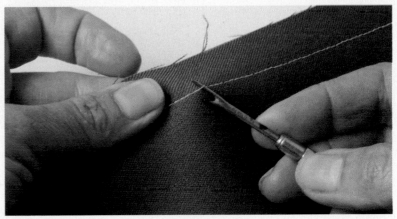

*Break stitches along one side of the seam with the narrow point of the seam ripper.*

*One easy way to finish a seam is with pinking shears. Pink the edges, trimming a small slice of fabric away from the seam allowance.*

## SEAMS FOR BIAS-CUT SKIRTS

Cut, making 1½-in. seams to allow the fabric to relax. Mark the seamline with basting. Press the pieces.

Pin along the marked seamline and try on the garment. Adjust where necessary. You may need to make smaller seam allowances to compensate for the pieces' having stretched slightly in length and contracted in width.

Sew with a slightly shorter stitch length than usual, stretching the fabric as you sew. Because bias does not ravel, you won't need to finish the seams.

# Finishes for Side Seams

Aim for simple, light, unobtrusive seam finishes. Test fabric scraps to see which seam finish is most compatible with your fabric. The seam finish should keep the seam edges from fraying and shouldn't show from the right side. If your fabric doesn't ravel, the best seam finish is none at all.

**Pinked Seams** Trimming with pinking shears is a classic, honest way to finish a seam (see photo, left). The ultimate in simplicity, it adds no bulk and won't show from the right side. After you sew the seam, trim away the smallest amount of fabric possible.

Test the pinking shears on fabric scraps first. On some fabrics, you can trim both layers of the seam allowance at one time. With other fabrics, to get a clean edge, you must open the seam allowance and trim single layers. Test both methods and compare the results.

Some pinking shears have a notched tip that will cut all the way to the end of the cut. Other brands work best if you don't fully open the shears and if you don't cut all the way to the points. Test to see how deep a cut you need to make to work smoothly.

There's also a rotary cutter with a wavy blade that works well as a pinking tool.

A pinked-and-stitched edge is especially flat and ravel-resistant: Sew a line of stitching 1/4 in. from the edge before the seam is sewn. Pink the edges after seaming, without cutting the line of stitching.

**Zigzag Seams** Zigzag edges are quick and simple finishes. Both are made after the seam is sewn and pressed.

Both finishes have two disadvantages, however. First, the extra stitching and thread can add bulk to thin fabrics, which will keep them from lying flat. Second, these finishes, which aren't found in ready-to-wear, shout "homemade." I generally don't use them, but you might want to experiment with them yourself.

For a zigzag finish, use a stitch of medium width and length. Stitch near the edge, but not along it, and trim close to the stitching. If your machine has this option, try a machine-overcast stitch. Stitch close to the edge so the points of the stitches fall almost at the edge of the fabric.

**Serged Seams** The serger, or overlock machine, has transformed home sewing. Although it doesn't replace a conventional machine, a serger is very useful for quickly cutting and finishing seam edges in one fast and easy operation (above right).

Fuse interfacings to pockets and zipper areas before serging. If your fabric frays easily, serge all around the skirt, but on more stable fabrics, serge only the seams that will be pressed open. Serge the hem after you mark the length and trim to desired width.

When using a serger, it's not necessary to cut wider seams than

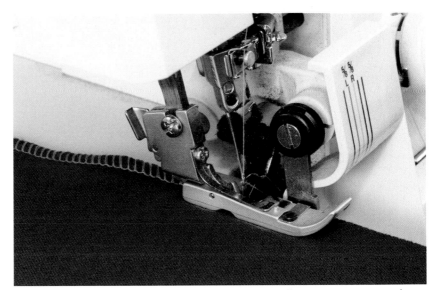

*A serger cuts and overcasts the edges of the seam allowance in one quick and easy operation.*

you normally would. The cutting edge of the serger trims just the ravelly edges before overcasting.

Use fine, soft thread, machine-embroidery thread, or texturized nylon to minimize the amount of thread impression "striking through" on the right side of the fabric. A 3-thread edge, using long staple polyester or coned "serger" thread, is the most versatile of the serged finishes. Or, if your machine has a 2-thread finish, try that for a flatter edge.

Serge a wide edge on fabrics that are heavy or bulky, and a narrow edge on flat fabrics that are lightweight to midweight.

# Finishes for Hems and Waistband Seams

For a flat and professional-looking finish, you can bind hems and waistband seams with a Hong Kong finish or with a rayon seam binding.

**_Hong Kong Finish_**  The Hong Kong finish is a simple and elegant touch for medium to heavy fabrics. This flat, narrow binding makes a fine finish for hems or an inside waistband seam on a skirt (see photo on p. 52), but it's too bulky for most side seams.

A Hong Kong finish has two lines of stitching and adds three layers of fabric to the edge. The seam edge is bound in bias strips of a lightweight fabric, such as China silk, rayon lining, silk, or polyester crepe de chine.

For the binding, cut 1¼-in. wide bias strips, piecing the lengths as necessary. Press the bias strips to remove excess stretchability and to prevent them from rippling.

Before you stitch the waistband to the skirt, sew the binding to the seam edge, with right sides together, ¼ in. from the edges. (Bind the hem in the same way after marking and trimming it.)

Trim the seam edge to an even ⅛ in. using sharp long-blade shears or a rotary cutter (**1**).

Wrap the binding around the seam edge and press. On the right side of the fabric, stitch in the "ditch" of the seam of the waistband and the binding—that is, where the two fabrics are sewn together (**2**). For accuracy, use an edgestitching foot with the needle in the center position.

On the wrong side of the fabric, trim the excess binding ⅛ in. from the stitching line (**3**). Bias doesn't fray, so the binding won't ravel.

**_Rayon Seam Binding_**  A flat woven-tape seam binding creates a dressmaker's touch for bulky and flat fabrics that ravel. Use rayon rather than polyester—it's softer, flatter, and more fluid. With just a bit of practice, you'll find this technique fast and simple.

Rayon seam binding adds less bulk than the Hong Kong finish. It has only one line of stitching and adds only two layers of fabric to the edge. This seam binding can also be used to finish the inside waistband edge and the hem edge.

Press the binding in half lengthwise, making one half slightly wider than the other. Hold the end in place with a straight pin as you work.

Position the narrow half of the binding on top of the right side of the fabric and stitch along this half (**4**). This way, you'll be sure that your stitches will catch the wider half of the binding on the other side of the fabric.

As you stitch along the edge of the binding, pull it slightly toward the fabric with your finger so that it wraps around and encases the raw edge. Press to eliminate puckers.

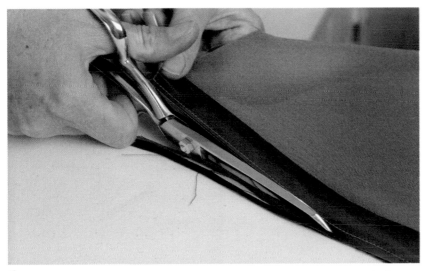

**1** *To apply Hong Kong finish, trim the binding to an even ⅛ in. with shears or a rotary cutter.*

**2** *Wrap the binding around the edge, press, and stitch in the ditch of the seam on the right side of the fabric.*

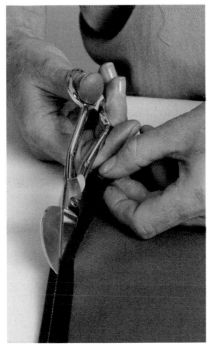

**3** *Trim excess binding on the wrong side of the fabric. Here, the author is using appliqué scissors to get as close as possible to the seam.*

**4** *To apply rayon seam binding, stitch the pressed binding with the narrower half on top of the right side of the fabric.*

# Darts, Pleats, and Gathers

*Darts, pleats, and gathers add dimension to a flat piece of fabric, sculpting and shaping it into curves and contours. With careful fitting, their placements and lines can emphasize and flatter your figure.*

# Darts

Darts are most often used to shape the back of the skirt. A fitted, darted front shows every bump and curve of the body. If you don't have a flat tummy, front darts may not be flattering and can be eliminated with a stitching technique called staystitch plus (p. 60).

When making darts, careful marking and stitching go hand in hand. Position pins all along the stitching line, with one horizontal pin marking the tip of the dart. Make sure that pins are in straight lines along both legs of the dart.

Stitch from the wide end of the dart, backstitching as you begin in order to secure the stitches **(1)**. Remove the pins as you come to them.

When you're ½ in. from the tip of the dart, change to a short stitch length (1.5mm) and stitch the last few stitches along the edge of the fabric. Shorter stitches increase stitching accuracy and make tying knots or backstitching unnecessary. Stitch evenly off the edge to prevent a bubble from forming at the tip of the dart **(2)**.

Sew a smooth and true dart every time by mentally drawing a line from the first stitches to the tip, pointing the machine in that direction. This visualization is helpful even if you've marked the stitching line with chalk.

Press the dart on a ham. A perfectly pressed dart is nearly invisible on the right side of the fabric.

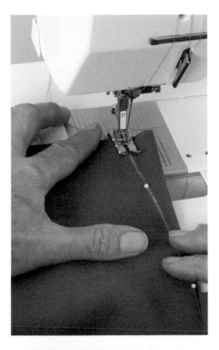

**1** *Begin by backstitching at the wide end of the dart.*

**2** *When you've reached the tip of the dart, stitch evenly off the fabric.*

# STAYSTITCH PLUS

Staystitch plus (also called easestitch plus) is a machine-stitching technique with a lot of uses. For example, instead of sewing the front darts of a skirt, you can simply ease the fullnessinto the waistband for a more flattering effect. Staystitch plus can be used to ease any skirt to fit into any other waistband.

All sewing machines are designed to sew two or more layers of fabric. Staystitch plus works with the machine's tendency to draw up fabric when sewing one layer.

To staystitch-plus, you stitch through one layer of fabric, applying pressure from behind to force a tiny bit more fabric into each stitch. Position your finger behind the foot to crimp the fabric and ease it through smoothly and evenly. Sew in sort segments, raising foot every few inches to release fabric.

Stitch short segments of fabric—1 in. to 2 in. at a time—then release the piled-up fabric by raising the presser foot (**1**).

When you're done, the skirt should be nearly equal in width to the pattern piece with the darts pinned into position (**2**). If you need to ease more fabric, make a second line of staystitch plus just inside the first line.

In order to develop an even, smooth tension while easing the fabric the correct amount, you'll need to experiment and practice.

**1** *As you force more fabric into each stitch by positioning your finger behind the foot, raise the presser foot every few inches to release the eased fabric.*

**2** *After you have used staystitch plus, the garment piece should be equal in width to the pattern piece with the darts pinned in place.*

# Pleats

Pleats add controlled fullness to skirts. They can be soft or sharp, placed all around the waist or hip, positioned in the front and/or the back, or used as details (as a kick pleat, for example).

If possible, make the pleats before sewing the side seams.

Mark the pleats with tailor's tacks (p. 49). Use two colors of embroidery floss: one for the fold of the pleat, the other for the placement line.

**Soft Pleats** Soft pleats must be secured accurately to hang gracefully. Hand- and machine-baste to keep them from shifting during fitting and construction. When the waistband is applied, the pleats are permanently stitched in place.

Pin the pleats into position, aligning the snip marks and tailor's tacks (1).

Hand-baste them securely well above and below the seamline with silk thread. Next, machine-baste them within the lines of hand-basting, above and below the seamline (2).

After stitching the first line of stitching for the waistband, set the pleats by steam-pressing them over the ham.

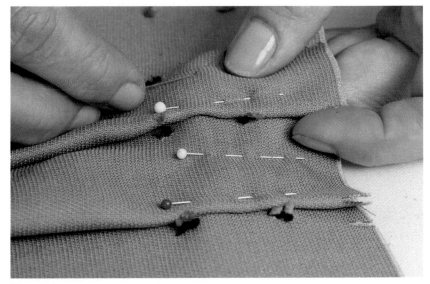

1 *Pin the soft pleats into position, aligning marks and tailor's tacks.*

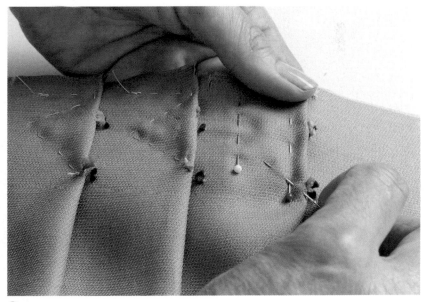

2 *Hand-baste the pleats in position above and below the seamline.*

**Sharp Pleats** Making sharp pleats requires care and accuracy.

Stitching close to the edge of a pleat keeps the pressed edges crisp and lasting, even in soft fabrics. You can edgestitch sharp pleats on the outside and/or inside of the garment. It's crucial to maintain the straight of the grain along the edge of long, straight pleats.

Mark the pleat fold line and placement lines with tailor's tacks every 3 in. to 4 in. Snip-mark at the fabric edges.

Press the pleats into position on a pressing surface long enough to support the length of the garment and wide enough to support several pleats (**1**).

Hand-baste the pleats with silk thread to secure them (**2**).

1  *Press sharp pleats into position on a long work surface.*

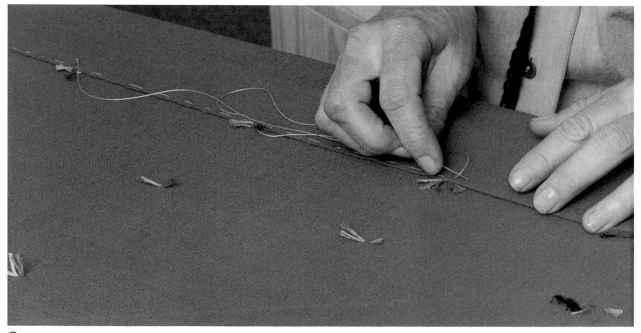

2  *Hand-baste the pleats securely with silk thread.*

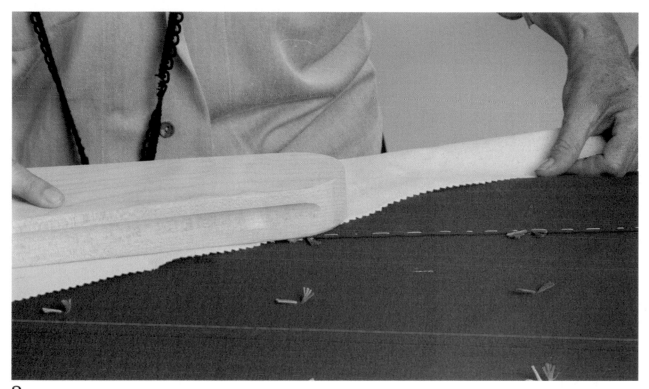

**3** *Use the clapper and a heavy press cloth to sharpen pleats in a pleated skirt.*

Press again on the wrong side of the fabric, using the clapper and a heavy press cloth to sharpen the pleat edges **(3).** Press again, finishing and touching up, on the right side of the fabric.

For a crisp finish, after the skirt is hemmed, you can edgestitch the inside edge, outside edge, or both edges of the entire pleat, on the wrong side of the garment **(4).**

Edgestitching adds weight and crispness, and holds the pleats in position. Use an edgestitching foot for greatest accuracy and speed. Always press again after edgestitching.

Another option is to edgestitch just the inside of the pleat within the hem. Again, stitch on the wrong side of the garment to conceal the stitches.

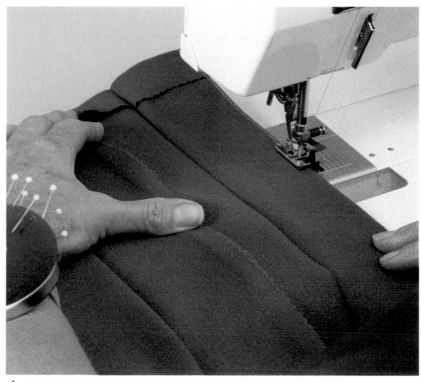

**4** *Edgestitching on the wrong side of the garment holds the crisp pleats in position.*

# Gathers

The best machine gathers imitate finely done hand shirring by creating even, flowing, vertical folds in a soft fabric. This kind of gathering is flattering to most figures. By positioning well-made gathers in the flatter parts of the body, you can create a slimming effect. Poorly done gathering, however, is uneven and lumpy and adds bulk to the figure.

One of the secrets of success is choosing the right fabric. Another is using three rows of gathering stitches rather than the traditional two. Careful stitching, pinning, and seaming are also essential.

On all sewing machines, the bobbin tension is adjusted to create a perfect stitch from the right side, so it's easiest to gather fabric by pulling the bobbin thread. Stitch on the right side of the fabric and use heavier thread in the bobbin to prevent the thread from breaking.

Test for the best stitch length. For even gathers, use the shortest stitch length that gathers with ease— generally, 3.5 to 4.5mm. Use a longer stitch with heavier fabrics.

If the gathers go all around the skirt, it's best to make them after sewing the side seams. If they don't, you can make them before sewing the side seams.

When making the gathers, stitch three parallel rows $7/8$ in., $3/8$ in., and $1/4$ in. from the edge of the fabric. The row farthest from the edge secures the gathers in position until you attach the waistband. (For smoother gathers in "challenging" fabrics, such as denim, stitch four rows.)

Test your fabric to be sure that the needle holes disappear after you've removed the gathering threads and steamed the gathers. If marks remain, make additional rows of stitching within the seamline to conceal them.

Start and stop stitching each row in the same place. Do not backstitch the ends or you won't be able to pull the threads easily later. Keep threads from tangling by cutting the upper threads 2 in. from the fabric.

Before you gather the skirt to fit the waistband, mark the skirt at center front, side seams, and center back. Also mark the waistband at the corresponding points. Pull the bobbin threads firmly but gently to gather the skirt.

When gathering a lot of fabric, divide and conquer:

- Section the area to be gathered into halves or quarters, marking carefully and clearly with chalk or snip marks. (Pins can fall out.)

- Gather each section separately.

Secure the thread ends by wrapping them in a figure eight around the pins at each end of the lines of stitching (**1**). Divide each gathered area in half repeatedly, forming small vertical folds, and pin the gathered sections securely with pins placed close together. Use a pin point to adjust the gathers so that they are evenly distributed (**2**).

The row of stitching that attaches the skirt to the waistband holds the carefully adjusted gathers permanently in position. Stitch on the wrong side of the fabric, adjusting the fabric folds as you work to prevent distortion (**3**). Stitch slowly. It's inevitable that you'll nick the machine needle with a pin as you stitch, so change the needle when you finish.

Check the evenness of the gathers on the right side of the garment before removing the gathering stitches. Be sure to remove all the threads before pressing—they can create stiffness and bulk in the seam allowance.

Pressing adds a final touch. First, press the seam flat as sewn. Next, work in sections on the wrong side, positioning the gathers over the ham. Set the gathers with steam so they lie even, gently pulling them lengthwise to create parallel folds (**4**). Be careful not to flatten them as you work.

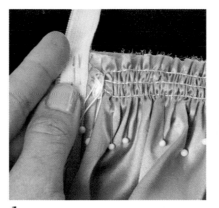

**1** *Secure the gathering threads by wrapping them in a figure eight around a straight pin. Divide and pin each gathered section to form a series of vertical folds.*

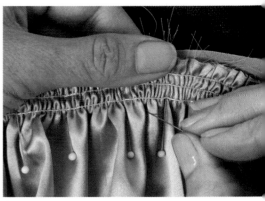

**2** *Adjust the gathers evenly with a pin point.*

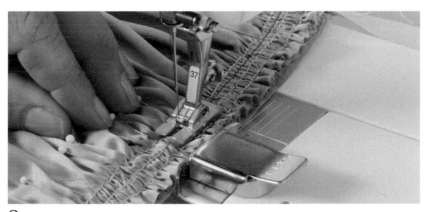

**3** *On the wrong side of the fabric, stitch the gathered skirt to the waistband. A magnetic seam guide ensures a straight line of stitching.*

**4** *Steam-press the gathers lightly over the ham.*

Trimming or grading gathers usually isn't necessary. If you do trim them, however, never trim closer than $3/8$ in. Any more than that and the gathered fabric edges will stand up stiffly, like a crewcut.

# Side-Seam Pockets

*Side-seam pockets, the easiest to sew, are a good first pocket for the beginner to master.*

Side-seam pockets work best on semi-fitted, full, and flared skirts with soft pleats or gathers. Don't use them on skirts that are very fitted at the waist and hip, pleated, or cut on the bias, however.

If your pattern does not have a pocket, adding this one is simple. Add $1/8$ in. extra at each side seam to make sure that the skirt has enough ease at the hip and high hip to accommodate a pocket. If the skirt is too snug, the pocket openings will gap.

When making a skirt with pockets, pin-fit carefully, baste the pocket opening before stitching, and press the garment well so that the pockets lie smooth and flat without bulges or bulk.

## Construction

You can keep pocket openings firm and stable by reinforcing the front opening with fusible tricot. (You don't need to reinforce the back of the pocket opening because it doesn't get stretched from use.) Mark its placement on skirt front.

Measure from the waist to $1/2$ in. below the bottom of the pocket opening. Cut a 1-in. wide strip of fusible tricot to this length for each pocket.

Fusible tricot is stable on the lengthwise grain and won't stretch. (Fusibles do stretch on the cross grain, however, so cut carefully.)

On the skirt front, position and fuse the interfacing over the seam so that it extends ¼ in. beyond the fold of the pocket opening **(1)**. This both strengthens and softens the edge.

Stitch the pocket to the side seam, using a ¼-in. seam allowance. You can also combine straight stitching with serged edges. Press the seam toward the pocket.

Stitch the side seams of the garment, working from the hem, until you reach the bottom of the pocket opening. Backstitch. Don't cut the thread. Instead, lift the pressure foot, carry the thread across, and reposition the needle at the top of the pocket opening **(2)**. Backstitch again and sew the rest of the seam. You can also change to a longer stitch and baste across the pocket opening rather than carrying the thread.

Press open the side and pocket seams as shown in the photo on the following page **(3)**, using the flat side of the ham if the hip area is curved. Use the clapper to smooth and flatten the pocket edges.

Topstitching gives the pocket opening a crisp finish. Mark the topstitching line for each pocket opening on the skirt front with a C-Thru ruler and erasable chalk or silk thread. Or you can simply stitch ¼ in. to ½ in. from the edge of the pocket opening, using the fold as a guide. With a slightly longer stitch, topstitch along the opening, backstitching at each end.

**1** *Mark notches on pocket and skirt seam.*

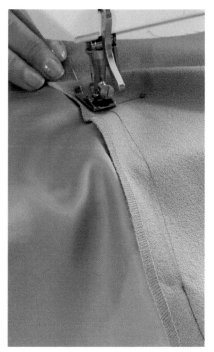

**2** *When stitching the side seams, backstitch the bottom of the pocket opening, carry the thread across the opening, backstitch the top, and continue the seam.*

Working from top to bottom, serge the outside and top edges of the pocket halves. Fuse the interfacing. Then, in one operation, beginning at the hem, stitch and finish the garment's side seams while attaching the pocket.

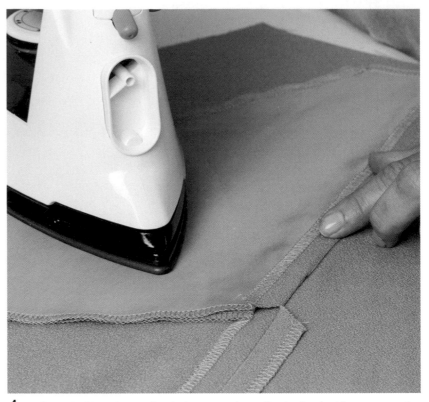

**3** *Press open the side seams and pocket seams.*

**4** *Before stitching the pocket halves together, clip the back side seam on the diagonal and press the back of the pocket to the front of the skirt.*

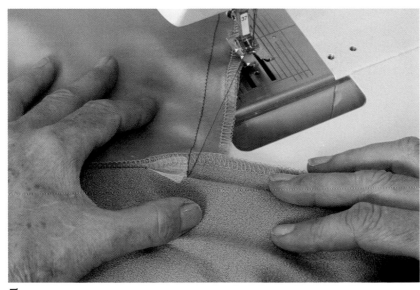

**5** *Sew the pocket together, beginning and ending at the pocket opening.*

Working over a ham, press the back of the pocket toward the front of the garment. Clip the back side seam so that the pocket will fall to the front of the garment easily (**4**). (Clipping on the diagonal prevents fraying.)

To assemble the halves of the pocket, stitch around the edges, beginning and ending at the backstitching that marks the pocket opening (**5**). Pinking is a fast, simple solution to finishing the pocket edges if you don't have a serger. Press the finished pocket to the front of the garment.

# SIDE-POCKET VARIATION

This side pocket doubles as a skirt opening. Not only does it eliminate the need for a zipper, it also adds a soft and functional design element. (Ralph Lauren uses side-pocket openings in his skirts.)

To turn a side-seam pocket into a side-pocket opening, make a mark 9 in. below the waist along the long curved edge of the pocket. Reinforce 1 in. on either side of the mark and clip to it, being careful not to cut through the reinforced stitching.

Construct the pockets as described on pp. 66-68, but leave the one on the left side of the garment open

above the mark. Finish this pocket opening by pressing the edge under ¼ in., and then another ¼ in. Topstitch on the right side.

Mark the left side seam on the waistband. Measure the pocket underlap—that is, the top of the pocket back from the side seam to the pocket edge. Add the length of the underlap plus two seam allowances to the finished waistband length.

Attach the waistband as you normally would and add closures (pp. 102-103), positioning them so that when the skirt is closed, the pocket halves align.

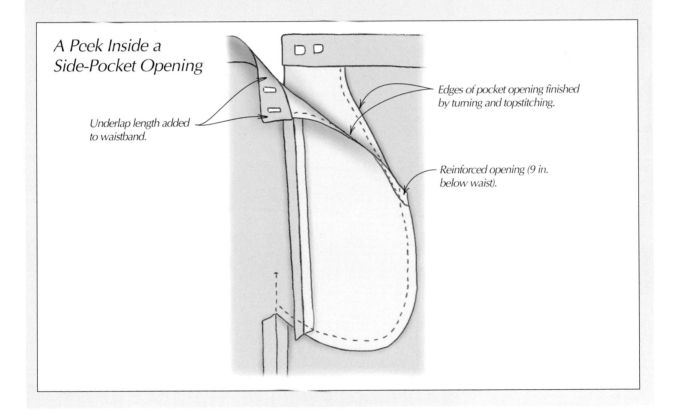

*A Peek Inside a Side-Pocket Opening*

*Underlap length added to waistband.*

*Edges of pocket opening finished by turning and topstitching.*

*Reinforced opening (9 in. below waist).*

# Kick Pleats and French Vents

*Kick pleats and French vents allow you more freedom of movement when wearing a slim-fitting skirt, and they are versatile design details as well.*

Kick pleats are stitched, closed pleats and French vents are faced openings. A kick pleat is positioned at the hemline to make a slim-fitting skirt more comfortable for you to move and walk in. A traditional closed kick pleat can be adapted to an open slit, frequently used by French designers and called a French vent (p. 72).

Keep your eye on the length, stitching, and placement of kick pleats and French vents in ready-to-wear garments so you can adapt your favorite skirt pattern. You can add them to any seam—center back, center front, or side.

Converting a pattern to create a kick pleat or French vent is done in the same way. Determine the finished length of the pleat or vent—don't forget to include the hem length. A good finished standard width is 3 in., including seam allowances. Add a scrap of tissue to the pattern and draw in the pleat or vent, adding the desired length and width to the seamline. The top of the opening can be left square or angled. Mark the seamlines. Make a dot at the top of the opening—this is where the stitching ends for a French vent and marks the pivot point for a kick pleat.

Add the kick pleat or French vent to the pattern first, then add the right amount of walking ease (p. 35).

1 *Apply a square of reinforcement at the top of both sides of the pleat opening.*

2 *Stitch from the square to the end of the extension and backstitch to reinforce.*

## Kick Pleat

Before sewing a kick pleat, always reinforce both sides of the top of the pleat opening to keep the fabric from tearing and the stitches from pulling out.

Position or fuse a 1-in. square of fusible or woven interfacing, a strip of tailor's tape (twill tape), or even a scrap of lining selvage at the top of both sides of the vent opening on the wrong side of the fabric **(1)**. Stitch the garment's seam to the square and press the seam in the direction it's sewn. With small reinforcing stitches, stitch from the square to the edge of the extension and backstitch **(2)**.

Fold back the extension on one side of the seamline and press it. Lay the other extension on top of the folded one, aligning the edges **(3)**. On the topmost layer, make a diagonal clip through the seam allowance to the reinforcement

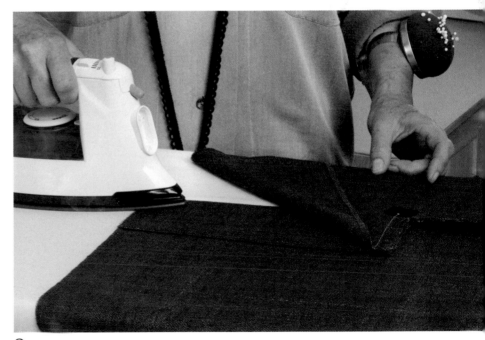

3 *Fold one extension and press it. Lay the other over it, aligning edges. Baste them into position at top of the extension.*

4 *To secure the open edge of the kick pleat invisibly, catchstitch on the inside of the garment.*

square to keep the garment's seam free and flat. Pin the layers into positon and baste at top along the stitching line.

Lift the garment pieces to double-check the hang of the kick pleat and correct as needed.

Press the skirt's seam open to the opening. To secure the open edge of the pleat, catchstitch on the inside of the garment (4) so that the stitches are invisible, or topstitch it on the right side of the garment to add extra detail.

# French Vent

The French vent is easier to construct and less likely to wrinkle than the kick pleat.

The extensions that form a kick pleat or French vent are the same and both are cut and reinforced in the same way. The difference is that on the French vent the extensions are pressed to either side of the opening, rather than overlapped on one side.

After the garment's seam is sewn and pressed, press the opening as shown, allowing the fabric to form straight folds that meet at the center (1).

**Mitering the Corner** For a beautiful inside finish, especially in a lined skirt, finish off the French vent with a mitered corner. (Before you try it on your garment, however, I recommend you practice mitering first with paper, and then make two samples with a stable fabric.)

Mark the hem length and fold line of the vent opening (2). Turn the marked edges under and press.

At the intersection of the hemline and the vent line, fold the fabric back at an angle, aligning the marked lines on top of each other (3). Press the folded corner. Trim a 1/4-in. seam allowance (4).

Fold the corner again, right sides together, to align the hem line with the vent line (5). Machine-stitch along the edge of the layers. Turn the mitered corner to its right side with a point turner and press the corner to form crisp edges.

**1** *On a French vent, the extensions are folded back on either side of the opening and pressed.*

**2** *To miter a corner, mark and press the hem and vent fold line.*

**3** *Fold the corner back, aligning the marked lines on top of each other, and press.*

**5** *Fold again and stitch right sides together. Turn the mitered corner to its right side with a point turner.*

**4** *Trim the folded corner to allow a ¼-in. seam allowance.*

Kick Pleats and French Vents **73**

# Zippers

*Zippers may be lapped, centered, or "invisible." Conquer the lapped zipper first. It has only one visible line of stitching, and it's perfect for skirts with a side or back opening.*

# Some Tips

- If this is your first zipper, or if you're using a challenging fabric, make three samples before putting the zipper in the garment. Keep the samples for later reference.

- I prefer to make the zipper openings longer than the pattern suggests—9 in. rather than the usual 7 in.

- I also like to use a zipper that is longer than the opening to ensure that the zipper closes in the waistband (especially good for raised and contoured waistbands).The longer opening also makes it easier to get into and out of the skirt. Cut off any excess zipper from the top after sewing the first seam on the waistband.

- Already prepared zippers are sturdier than those sold by the yard. Strong and flexible polyester zippers are preferable to metal ones.

- A zipper foot is essential. It allows you to machine-stitch close to the zipper, whereas the bulky regular foot gets in the way.

- Put the zipper in while the garment is flat. This isn't always the order of construction recommended by most pattern directions, but it's easier. If you're using a side-seam zipper, fit and adjust the side seams before inserting the zipper.

- Contrary to most directions, don't baste the zipper opening closed before you put in the zipper. Simply press the seam allowances under—you'll have more control and you'll be able to make sure the zipper teeth are covered.

- Add interfacing behind the zipper as you would for a pocket (p. 67). This little-known secret makes a noticeable difference. It stabilizes the fabric and makes the final, visible stitching easier.

I recommend a fusible tricot, such as Sof-Knit. Work with ¾-in. strips cut on the straight of the grain to stabilize the fabric and add body, and strips cut on the bias or cross grain for soft shaping. (Keep a supply of scraps on hand to save some time.)

- It's hard to visualize the ⅝-in. seamline at the waistline, so mark it with snips. Beginners may also benefit from marking the seamline along the zipper opening with chalk after the interfacing is fused.

- Press curves on the ham (as on a side-seam zipper, for example) over the flattest curve for subtle, rounded shaping. Press a side seam over a ham; press a center-back seam flat.

## HAND-BASTING

Hand-basting is very effective for holding the zipper in position as you machine-stitch, as well as for marking stitching lines in other parts of the garment.

Use a single strand of silk thread, especially with delicate or slippery fabrics, such as silk or velvet. Silk thread won't show when you press it or leave a trail of fibers when you remove it.

As you hand-stitch, use the basting thread itself as a guide. Hold the thread taut and parallel to the edge of the fold, and sew along it. Machine-stitch next to the hand-basting.

To mark straight stitching lines, use an erasable chalk, such as Clo-chalk, which disappears within 48 hours or washes out. (Always test marking tools on your fabric before you use them.)

**1** *Fuse interfacing to the zipper's seam allowances. Stitch the skirt's seam to the bottom of the opening.*

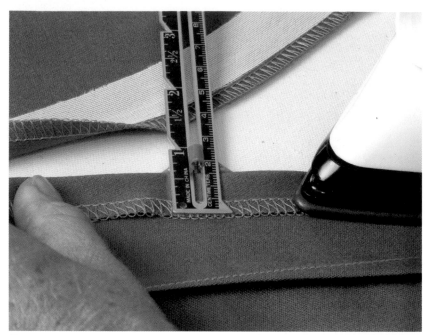

**2** *Turn and press the seam allowance for the overlap to a width of ⅝ in.*

**3** *Turn and press the seam allowance for the underlap to a width of ½ in., forming a slight pleat at the bottom of the opening.*

# Lapped Zipper

A lapped zipper laps left over right. An easy way to remember this is to visualize how it will look when finished: On the right side of the garment, the lap that conceals the zipper will be on the left side of the seam.

Snip-mark the seam allowance at the waist. Transfer the mark for the bottom of the zipper opening from the pattern onto the fabric by marking it with a snip at the edge of the seam allowance or with a chalk line.

Apply ¾-in. wide strips of interfacing that are ½ in. longer than the zipper opening. Position them so that they extend beyond the bottom mark for the zipper and ⅛ in. to ¼ in. beyond the seamline into the seam allowance. Fuse the strips to the fabric.

Sew the garment's seam up to the zipper opening, and backstitch to reinforce the end **(1)**. Press the seam open.

Press open the seam allowance for the overlap to a width of ⅝ in. **(2)**. On a side-seam zipper, this is the seam allowance toward the front of the garment; on a center-back zipper, this is the seam allowance on the left side of the seamline.

Press open the underlap seam allowance to a width of ½ in. **(3)**. Form a ⅛-in. pleat at the bottom of the underlap while pressing.

Close the zipper and, with it face up, position the stop ¼ in. to ⅜ in. above the bottom of the opening. Pin or hand-baste the zipper to the underlap, keeping the teeth of the zipper next to the fold. With a zipper foot, machine-stitch from bottom to top, a scant ⅛ in. from the folded edge (4).

With the zipper still closed, pin the overlap in position on the right side of the garment. Be sure to align the snips that mark the seam allowance at the waist (5). The overlap edge should just cover the underlap stitching. Allow extra fabric at the top to accommodate the bulk of the pull tab.

Hand-baste the overlap in position, making sure it just covers the zipper and the pull tab. (It's helpful to pull the tab down a few inches and finish basting with the top of the zipper open.)

Mark and hand-baste the topstitching line slightly to the side of the final machine-stitching line (about ⅜ in. to ½ in. from the folded edge). Check to make sure the basting stitches catch all the layers of fabric and the zipper.

Close the zipper. Starting at the seam at the bottom of the opening, backstitch, then take about five to seven stitches across to the basted line. Pivot and topstitch from bottom to top along the line of basting (6). You can also stitch by hand if you prefer (p. 79).

Avoid a curve in the topstitching around the pull tab by stopping 2 in. from the top of the opening, opening the zipper, and then continuing a smooth topstitching line to the waistline (7).

**4** *Machine-stitch the basted zipper to the underlap using a zipper foot.*

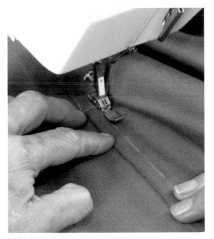

**6** *Hand-baste the topstitching on the overlap, and machine-stitch just outside the basting.*

**7** *To avoid an uneven topstitching line at top, open the zipper a few inches and finish stitching in a straight line.*

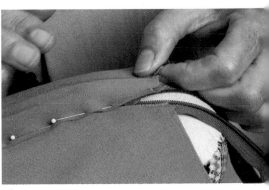

**5** *Pin the overlap in position, aligning the marks for the seam at the waist.*

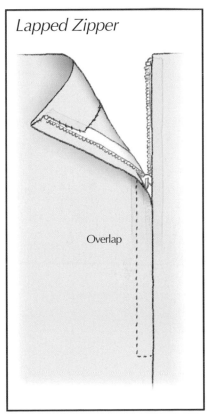

## Lapped Zipper

Overlap

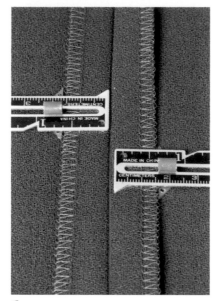

1 *Press ⅝-in. seam allowances on both sides of the zipper opening. (The raw edges of these garment pieces have already been serged.)*

# Centered Zipper

A centered zipper requires skill and precision to sew because it has two lines of topstitching, which must be straight, parallel to each other, and an equal distance from the seam. Symmetrical, centered zippers are a good choice for the back of a skirt.

The topstitching on a centered zipper is a scant ¼ in. to ⅜ in. from the opening. The fabric is slightly raised at the opening because the teeth and pull tab are completely covered when the zipper is closed. As for the lapped zipper, you can stitch by hand or topstitch by machine.

Snip-mark the seam allowance for the zipper at the waist, apply interfacing, and press open the seam at the zipper opening.

Stitch the garment's seam to the bottom of the zipper opening, backstitch to reinforce the stitching, and press the seam open. Press a ⅝-in. seam allowance on both sides of the zipper opening (1).

On the right side of the garment, pin the closed zipper through all thicknesses, forcing both sides of the fabric together slightly more than natural to form a ridge (2). The heavier the fabric, the more pronounced the ridge will be. When the zipper is sewn in, this

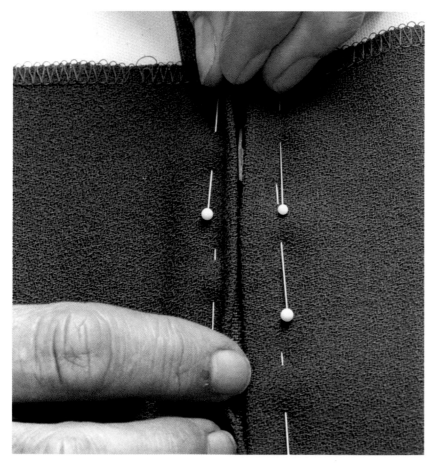

2 *Pin the closed zipper to the skirt opening, forcing both side of the fabric together slightly more than natural, so that a ridge is formed.*

## HAND-PICKED ZIPPER

For a fine custom touch, the final stitching on a centered or lapped zipper can be done by hand with a backstitch.

With a double strand of waxed sewing thread (or buttonhole thread for a more pronounced look), insert the needle through all the layers. Each stitch is formed backward, behind the point where the thread emerges. Make a stitch, then bring the needle through again ¼ in. to ⅜ in. in front of that stitch. From the right side, the stitching looks like tiny, evenly spaced dots in a straight line parallel to the fold.

It takes a bit of practice to develop a consistent, straight stitch length and tension. Try making a long sample before you topstitch the actual garment.

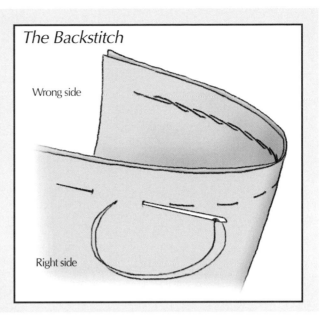

*The Backstitch*

Wrong side

Right side

ridge flattens out and covers the zipper teeth completely. You may need to open and close the zipper and reposition it more than once (double-sided basting tape makes the job easier). Pull the tab all the way up to be sure there's enough fabric to cover it at the waist end.

Hand-baste, just to one side of the topstitching line. With the zipper closed, begin topstitching at the seam at the bottom of the opening. Take about four stitches, pivot, and topstitch along one side of the opening to the waist. Backstitch to reinforce.

Again, begin at the seam at the bottom of the opening and topstitch the other side of the opening, from bottom to top (3). Backstitch.

Press the finished zipper on the right side of the garment, using a press cloth if necessary.

**3** *Begin at the bottom of the zipper opening and topstitch along each side to the top.*

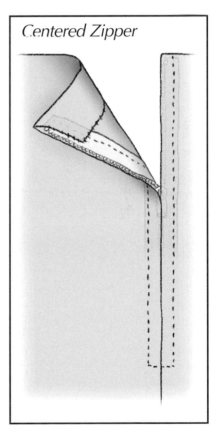

*Centered Zipper*

# Invisible Zipper

The invisible zipper is a specially made, thin and flexible zipper. It can be sewn right into the seam of a garment without topstitching. It's an easy zipper to sew, but if this zipper is entirely new to you, practice before you begin.

Invisible zippers work well with double-knits, velvet, and slippery or unstable fabrics. They're also perfect for bias skirts and for designs that look best without any visible stitching. Interfacing may not be necessary, except with lightweight fabric or bias. To be sure, test first.

You will need a special zipper foot made for invisible zippers and possibly a shank adapter for your machine.

Do not stitch the seam before you put in the zipper. Fuse the interfacing to the seam allowances (p. 76).

Mark the bottom of the opening on the unsewn seam and on the bottom of the zipper. If the zipper is too long, shorten it from the bottom. (The finished zipper will always end up about ½ in. shorter than you planned, so allow extra length as needed.)

To shorten the zipper, drop the feed dog and secure the end of the zipper with a wide zigzag stitch. Cut the zipper ¾ in. below the zigzag stitching (**1**).

Open the zipper. Working on the wrong side, press the zipper coils open with a warm iron.

With the zipper face down, pin the right side to the right side of the garment. Position the coils on the seamline (the edge of the zipper tape will be a scant ¼ in. from the raw edge); the bottom of the stop ½ in. below the mark for the bottom of the opening; and the top of the tape ¼ in. below the top edge of the fabric. Working from top to bottom, position the pins so you can easily pull them out as you stitch.

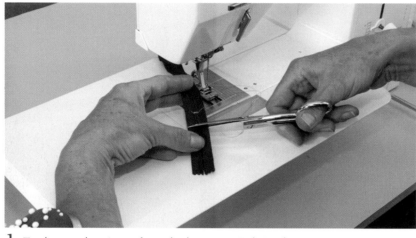

**1** *To shorten the zipper from the bottom, stitch in place, using zigzag stitching with the feed dog lowered, and cut off the excess zipper below the stitching.*

**2** *With the right side of the zipper tape to the right side of the fabric, stitch each half of the zipper from top to bottom.*

(You may want to machine-baste the zipper before you machine-stitch it in place.) If your fabric shifts easily (as do velvet and silkies) or needs matching (plaids and stripes), hand- or machine-baste first.

With the needle centered in the hole in the invisible-zipper foot and the left groove of the foot over the coil, stitch from top to bottom until the foot touches the stop (2). Backstitch at each end.

Close and open the zipper to make sure the stitching is not too close to the teeth, which would prevent it from unzipping easily, or too far away, which would cause the zipper to show.

With the zipper closed, position the right side of the other half of the zipper tape to the right side of the other half of the garment. Make sure the zipper halves align at the top of each side of the garment.

Open the zipper and stitch on the wrong side of the tape with the right groove of the zipper foot over the coil (3). Again, backstitch to reinforce the ends.

Close the zipper. Slide the zipper foot to the left so the needle goes through the outside notch. Holding the end of the zipper out of the way, stitch 2 in. beyond the zipper stop (4). Change back to your regular pressure foot and finish stitching the seam. Press.

Stitch the loose ends of the zipper to the seam allowances to secure them, being careful not to catch the garment. Press.

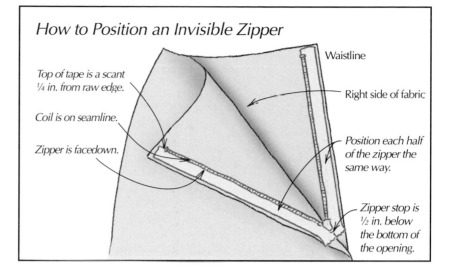

## How to Position an Invisible Zipper

Top of tape is a scant ¼ in. from raw edge.

Coil is on seamline.

Zipper is facedown.

Waistline

Right side of fabric

Position each half of the zipper the same way.

Zipper stop is ½ in. below the bottom of the opening.

**3** *Stitch the right side of the second half of the zipper to the right side of the second half of the garment.*

## Invisible Zipper

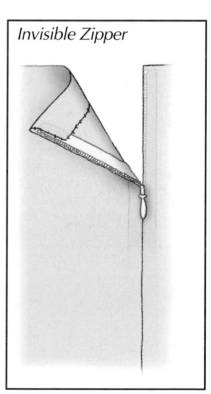

**4** *Hold the end of the zipper out of the way and stitch 2 in. below the zipper stop.*

# The Lining

*A lining finishes the inside of your garment, reduces wrinkles, and helps the skirt hang well.*

Skirt linings hang free of the skirt and are hemmed separately. They're attached at the waist, and the top edges are concealed by a waistband or facing.

Linings are secured to the garment by hand-stitching around the zipper (and the French vent opening, if there is one).

Sew the lining's side seams on a conventional machine or with a serger. To add a bit more ease, use a ½-in. seam allowance. Stitch the center-back seam, ending just below the zipper opening.

Backstitch to reinforce the ends of the stitching. Press the seams open. If there is a French vent, reinforce the corners and clip diagonally as you did for the garment **(1)**.

Don't sew darts in the lining. Instead, when you baste the lining to the waist, simply position and pin the darts as if they were tucks. The tuck is placed next to the dart, but it folds in the opposite direction to minimize bulk **(2)**.

**1** *If the skirt has a French vent, reinforce and clip the corners of the lining as you did for the garment.*

**2** *Don't make darts in the lining. Instead, make a tuck in the lining next to the dart in the skirt, but fold it in the opposite direction.*

## SEW, FIT, AND SEW

One of the secrets to a good fit is to continue to fine-tune the fit as you sew. (For this reason, always wear clothing that you can slip into and out of easily while you're working.)

Construct the front and back of the skirt separately so that you can fit the garment at the side seams.

Pin the side seams along the ⅝-in. seam allowance, wrong sides together, with pins parallel to and along the seamline. Mark the waistline with basting stitches so you can see it clearly. Wearing appropriate undergarments and shoes, try on the pinned skirt. Pin a 1-in.-wide piece of elastic around your waist to simulate a waistband. You can now adjust the side seams to fit your contours.

Let out or take in the seam as needed and try the skirt on again until the fit pleases you. With tailor's chalk, mark the alterations on the wrong side of the fabric. Draw a smooth line with the hip curve, making sure both side seams are the same.

The details and constructions methods for your specific skirt style will determine the best times for fitting as you sew. Make notes on the pattern instruction sheet (pp. 46-47).

Check again for swayback and ease at the waist before constructing the waistband or waistline facing. When you're making a classic, fitted waistband, try on the skirt again after the first row of stitching, and once more after the waistband finish is complete.

For skirts with contoured or raised waistbands, apply the facings to the front and back separately so you can fit them as you fit the side seams. This simplifies fitting and construction and makes any additional changes easier.

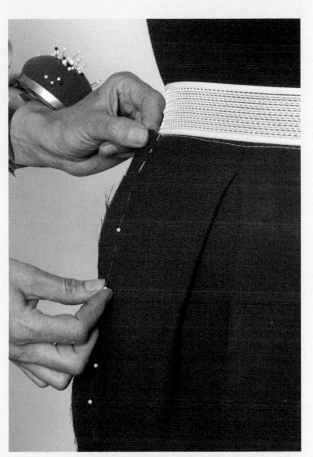

*Fit the skirt at the side seams by adjusting the seam allowances.*

Make all your adjustments, stitch, press, and try on the skirt yet again. It's not uncommon to redo a seam more than once! Continue fitting until you are satisfied.

Fitting is a trial-and-error process. The very best way to understand fitting is to just do it!

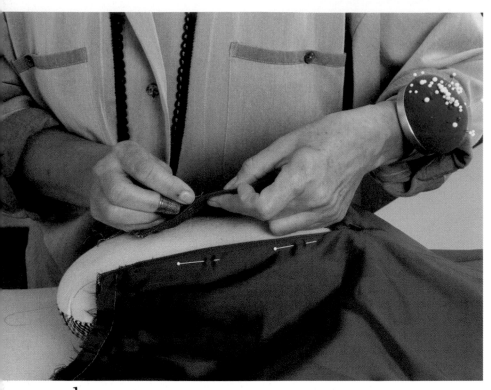

# Attaching the Lining

Insert the lining into the skirt with wrong sides together, and pin the side, center-back, and front seams. Fold tucks in the lining and pin them so they lie in the opposite direction to the skirt darts, as shown on p. 82.

Turn under and finger-press the seam allowance on each side of the zipper opening, making sure the lining won't get caught in the zipper teeth. Slipstitch the lining to the zipper tape (**1**).

Machine- or hand-baste the lining to the skirt ⅛ in. inside the waist seamline. Baste the lining to the waistband ½ in. from the waistband's edge.

Establish the hem length for the lining. How long you make it depends on how you plan to finish the bottom edge (as described on the facing page). Generally, the lining should be 1 in. shorter than the skirt. Press under the hem.

If your skirt has a French vent, you should have cut the lining as described on p. 36. Turn under and pin a ⅝-in. seam allowance in the lining and slipstitch loosely to attach it to the edges of the vent extensions (**2**).

**1** *Turn under the seam allowances and slipstitch the lining to the zipper tape. Make sure the lining fabric won't get caught in the teeth.*

**2** *If your skirt has a French vent, slipsitch the turned-under edge of the lining to the edges of the extensions.*

# Hemming the Lining

There are three options for finishing the hem edge of a skirt lining: serging, turning under, and trimming with lace.

If you decide to finish the edge with serging, be sure to cut the lining 1 in. shorter than skirt.

The hem can also be turned under ¼ in. to ½ in., turned again 1 in. to 2 in., and then topstitched. This creates a clean, strong finish. For this treatment, cut the lining the same length as the skirt.

For a simple couture touch, apply lace at the hem with a zigzag stitch (**1**). The lining will look and feel like a built-in slip (this was a signature feature of Jacqueline Kennedy's skirts when she was First Lady). You need to adjust the lining length to compensate for the width of the lace. In other words, cut the lining 1 in. shorter than the skirt length minus the width of the lace.

Trim the excess fabric under the lace close to the stitching (**2**).

**1** *To add an elegant couture touch, attach lace to the edge of the lining before hemming.*

**2** *After you have attached the lace, trim the excess close to the line of stitching.*

# Waistbands

*The waistline of a skirt can be finished in a variety of ways: from the simplest elastic casing to a precisely fitted, multilayered interfaced band.*

# PROFESSIONAL TIPS FOR APPLYING A WAISTBAND

Whichever waistband style you choose, the techniques for pinning, stitching, and pressing are the same. Here are some tips for getting frustration-free professional results.

• Pin the waistband to the skirt, right sides together, matching and pinning side seams and centers first. Ease the remaining fabric into the waistband and pin it in place. Position the pins on the seamline so they can be pulled out easily as you sew.

• Stitch with the wrong side of the waistband facing you so it's easier to see and control your work. When sewing a waistband to a gathered skirt, however, stitch with the gathered side up so you can be sure the gathers feed evenly into the machine.

• The waistband is smaller than the skirt, so the action of the machine will do some of the easing for you. If the fabric resists easing, however, hold it at a vertical angle as you sew—a factory trick that makes the job easier.

• Careful pressing is essential to the finished appearance of the waistband. Press the first, and most visible, seam flat as sewn, then press it toward the waistband. Unless the fabric is very heavy, you don't usually need to trim this seam allowance. Use a clapper to flatten as you press, and work over a ham as needed.

• To save time and ensure accuracy in the final stitching, after the ends have been finished, press the waistband as it will be sewn, shaping over the ham. As you press, place pins in the ditch of the seam, catching the back of the waistband, to hold the pressed shape.

• Your pattern will likely tell you simply to turn under the edge of the waistband before sewing it onto the skirt. There are four other, less bulky ways to finish the waistband edge:

1. Use the selvage edge as the finished edge.

2. Serge the edge.

3. Make a Hong Kong edge finish with a bias strip of lining the length of the waistband and 1 in. wide (p. 56).

4. Wrap the edge with a rayon seam binding (p. 56).

Skirts can be made with a pull-on elasticized waistband, which is especially easy for beginners to construct (p. 89); a classic fitted waistband (p. 92); a fitted elasticized waistband (p. 96); a contoured waistband (p. 99); or a raised waistband (p. 101). Some, but not all, require interfacings (pp. 93-95) and closures (pp. 102-103).

Commercial patterns usually provide basic instructions for attaching and interfacing a waistband, but you might want to adapt the pattern for one of these other alternatives.

# Fitting the Waist

A good fit at the waist is crucial to the overall fit and drape of the finished skirt. Ease, the difference between the wearer's body and the amount of fabric in the garment, determines how you will look and feel in the skirt—and ultimately whether or not you will wear it.

Think of your waist measurement, the finished waistband (or facing), and the waist seamline of the skirt as concentric circles, each nesting into the other. The finished waistband is larger than your waist to allow for movement, comfort, and enough room to tuck in a blouse. The waist seamline of the skirt is larger than the waistband so that, when the extra fabric is eased in, the skirt will still flow smoothly over the stomach and hips.

If the fit is right, there's enough ease for you to slip your thumb easily under the waistband. This same amount of ease is added to your waist measurement and determines the length of the finished waistband (excluding the underlap and seam allowances, which are added later).

The amount of recommended ease varies, depending on the style of the waistband and the figure—for example, slim figures generally require less ease than heavy ones. At the beginning of each section on the various waistband styles, you'll find the basic recommendation for the amount of ease for that style for the average figure. Although there are general guidelines, remember that ease is a matter of personal preference. Always measure your body or your favorite skirts to determine how much ease you'd like to have in your finished waistband, and adjust accordingly.

## CHECKING THE FIT

Before you apply the waistband, try on the skirt to double-check the fit of the garment.

Mark the waist seamline by machine-basting the skirt with thread of a contrasting color. Pin a 1-in. to 2-in. wide length of elastic in place as a temporary waistband. Adjust the skirt so that the lower edge of the elastic is positioned along the waist seamline. The elastic "waistband" should rest along your natural waist, with some ease—not too tight, not too loose. Fine-tune the position and fit.

If necessary, at this point, you can adjust for swayback if you didn't alter the pattern when pin-fitting (pp. 40-41).

Now remove the skirt and measure along the waist seamline, excluding the underlap and seam allowances. This measurement should be from 1½ in. to 2 in. greater than the length of the finished waistband. The extra skirt fabric will be eased into the waistband later.

If the skirt's waist measurement is less than 1½ in. or more than 2 in. greater than the waistband measurement, you have several options. You can take in or let out equal amounts of fabric at the side seams. You can also adjust the darts as necessary. If the skirt is too big, you can draw in the extra fabric by running a row or two of gathering stitching (using the next-to-longest machine stitch) and easing evenly. You can also use staystitch plus (p. 60), or a combination of both. If the skirt is big, your waist small, and your hips high and round, a fitted, elasticized waistband (p. 96) also provides a solution.

# Pull-on Waistband

**Amount of Ease:**
*Waistband length: Hip measurement plus 2 in. (plus 1¹⁄₄ in. for two ⁵⁄₈-in. seam allowances). The waist seamline should measure 2 in. more than the finished waistband.*

The pull-on waistband is a simple and professional detail that can be used with knits or lightweight wovens. This style of waistband slips on easily over the hips, but doesn't add bulk at the waist. You can even position pleats or gathers where you want them, while retaining the comfort and ease of a pull-on waistband.

Knit ribbing gives the best stretch and the least bulk. You can also use cross-grain knits or lengthwise or cross-grain wovens.

***Measure and Cut*** Cut the waistband to a length equal to your hip measurement plus 2 in. plus two ⁵⁄₈-in. seam allowances. The extra length will allow for those fabrics with zero stretch— for example, all wovens and some stable knits.

Cut the waistband wider than the finished width, and plan to trim it after you've stitched it to the garment. Knits, in particular, often become more narrow as they are stretched and stitched in place. For example, if I'm using 1¹⁄₄-in. wide elastic, I cut the waistband 4¹⁄₂ in. wide, which allows for two ⁵⁄₈-in. seam allowances and about

³⁄₄ in. of extra fabric. I trim the waistband to size and finish it after I've sewn the elastic to the seam allowance.

Cut the elastic 2 in. to 3 in. shorter than your waist measurement plus two ¹⁄₄-in. seam allowances. (I use flat-rib elastic or Ban-rol.)

To assemble the waistband, sew the seams and trim them to ¹⁄₄-in. allowances. Press them open and topstitch them at center with a wide zigzag stitch **(1)**. This will hold the seam flat and help you identify the garment's center back.

Divide the waistband in quarters, and mark each section. Pin the waistband to the garment, right

**1** *Sew the waistband together and topstitch with a wide zigzag stitch.*

2 *After dividing the waistband into quarters, pin it to the skirt, matching marks at centers and side seams.*

3 *Sew the waistband to the skirt, stretching it as needed to fit.*

sides together, at centers and at side seams (**2**).

Stitch on the wrong side of the waistband, stretching it as needed to fit the garment (**3**). If the garment is substantially larger than the waistband, on some fabrics (but rarely knits), you may need to use gathering stitches. Press the stitched seams toward the waistband.

Lap the seam allowances of the elastic to form a circle and stitch the ends with a serpentine or zigzag stitch (**4**). Trim the ends and divide the elastic into quarters, as you did the waistband.

Position the edge of the elastic next to the waistline stitching and pin the elastic to the seam allowance, matching the marks at center front, back, and side seams. Stitch the elastic to the seam allowance with a long, wide zigzag stitch, stretching as you stitch (**5**).

Wrap the waistband around the elastic. Trim width as needed, but be sure there will be enough fabric beyond the waistline stitching so that when you stitch on the right side, you'll catch the inside bottom edge of the waistband. Finish the waistband edge.

On the right side of the fabric, place pins in the ditch of the seam, positioning them so you can easily remove them as you sew (**6**). Pin or baste the waistband vertically at each quarter to prevent it from shifting during stitching. On the right side of the garment, stitch in the ditch to finish (**7**).

Another finishing option is to stitch several rows of topstitching, stretching as you sew. If you plan to topstitch, keep in mind that every row of stitching stretches the elasic about 1 in., so fit the elastic more snugly. Another trick is to use a longer stitch so as not to distort the elastic.

**4** *A wide serpentine stitch will secure the ends of the elastic and keep them lying flat.*

**5** *With the edge of the elastic next to the waistline stitching, stitch with a wide zigzag, stretching as you go.*

**6** *Working on the right side of the garment, place pins in the ditch, catching the inside bottom edge of the waistband.*

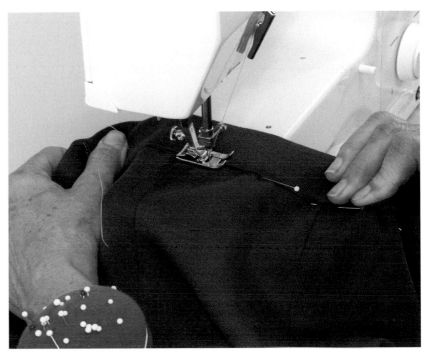

**7** *To finish the waistband, stitch in the ditch, as shown here, or topstitch several rows.*

## MAKE A FITTED WAISTBAND PATTERN

Once you have a comfortable waistband, file its measurements with your patterns. You can also make a permanent pattern piece to use with all your skirts.

To compute the length and width of a custom-fit waistband, start with your waist measurement (p.28). If your waist measures 26½ in. and you want 1½ in. of ease, your finished waistband measurement is 28 in. (**A**). If you use ½-in. seam allowances, double that amount (**B**). The underlap should be at least 1½ in. (**C**). For this waistband, the total length of fabric to cut is 30½ in.

| | |
|---|---|
| **A.** Finished length (waist measure + preferred amount of ease) | 28 in. |
| **B.** Seam allowances multiplied by 2 | 1 in. |
| **C.** Underlap (measure under fly, pocket extension, or simply use length you prefer) | 1½ in. |
| **Total cut length** | 30½ in. |

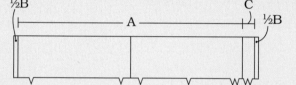

As a rule, waistbands are 1 in. to 2 in. wide. If you want your finished waistband to be 1¼ in. wide, multiply the finished width by two (**A**). If the front seam allowance is ⅝ in. (**B**), and you're using a selvage edge, Hong Kong finish, or rayon seam binding, add another ¼ in. to the back seam allowance (**C**). Always add another ¼ in. for turning under the inside edge of the fabric (**D**). The total cut width of this waistband is 3⅝ in.

| | |
|---|---|
| **A.** Finished width multiplied by 2 | 2½ in. |
| **B.** Front seam allowance | ⅝ in. |
| **C.** Back seam allowance (Add ¼ in. for selvage edge, Hong Kong finish, or seam binding.) | ¼ in. |
| **D.** Turn of cloth (extra fabric to go up and over the fold) | ¼ in. |
| **Total cut width** | 3⅝ in. |

# Classic Fitted Waistband

**Amount of Ease:**
*Waistband length: Waist measurement plus 1 in. to 1½ in. (plus 1¼ in. for two ⅝-in. seam allowances).*

---

The fitted waistband is a long rectangle cut on the lengthwise or crosswise grain, interfaced, and fitted with a minimum of ease.

Cutting it on the lengthwise grain with one edge on selvedge provides a finished edge that lies flat on the inside of the skirt. You can also create cross-grain and bias-grain waistbands by piecing at the side or back seams.

If your skirt has a lining, insert it before you construct and attach the waistband.

Use the commercial pattern for the waistband and make any necessary adjustments, or make your own custom-fit waistband. Be sure the b ody of the skirt is completed and fits well before you cut the waistband—in case any more alterations are needed.

Three interfacing options are described on pp. 93-95. Whichever you decide to use, finish the ends of the fitted waistband as described on p. 98. Apply closures as described on pp. 102-103.

**Marking**  With chalk, pins, or snips, mark the stitching lines, seam allowances, and underlap on the wrong side of the waistband. Match centers, forming a circle. Divide the circle into quarters that correspond to the skirt's center front and back and side seams.

The skirt doesn't divide neatly into four even quarters at the waistline. The back from side to side is ½ in. narrower than the front (this is true for women and men of any size and shape). Adjust the waistband after establishing the garment quarters. Take ¼ in. off the back at each side seam and add it to the center front to compensate for the difference from front to back. Shift the side-seam mark when pinning the waistband in place.

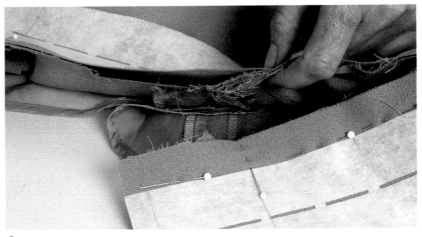

**1** *Cut the interfacing to the same length as the waistband, including seam allowances.*

# Three Interfacing Options for the Classic Waistband

Interfacing helps give a garment its shape, body, and support. The two types of interfacing are fusible and sew-in. Woven fusible interfacings designed for men's shirts and sold by the yard make good waistband interfacings.

***Fusible Interfacing*** Quick and easy to use, fusible interfacing is applied with a warm iron and requires no stitching. Nonwoven fusible interfacing has no grain. Packaged waistbanding is precut and sold in different widths, according to the width of the waistband. Whichever type you use, always fuse a swatch first to make sure the interfacing and the fabric are compatible in weight.

Precut fusible interfacing is perforated so the stitching lines and fold lines are easy to see; one half is ¼ in. smaller than the

other. Cut the interfacing to the same length as your waistband, including seam allowances (**1**). A small amount of interfacing in the seam will stabilize the end of the waistband.

Position the interfacing on the waistband, wrong side of fabric to adhesive side of interfacing. The narrower half forms the front of the waistband. Be sure the edge of the narrower half is ¾ in. from the raw edge of the fabric to allow space for stitching and for turning the fabric. Mark the seams, centers, and underlap on the narrow half. Fuse the interfacing to the fabric with a warm iron, following the manufacturer's instructions.

Staystitch-plus the skirt to fit the waistband (**2**). Pin the waistband to the skirt, wrong sides together, matching seams and centers and easing as needed.

With the waistband side toward you, stitch a ⅝-in. seam allowance, just inside the interfacing edge. Press.

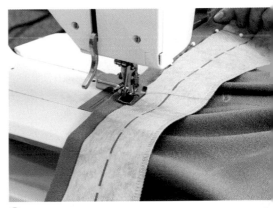

**2** *Staystitch-plus the waistline of skirt to fit the waistband.*

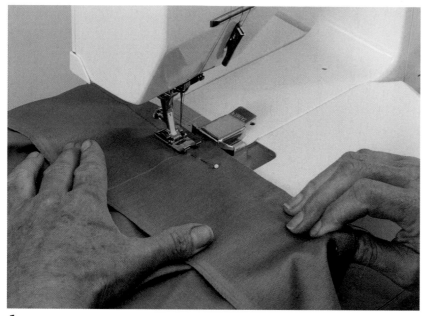

1 Stitch the waistband to the skirt, right sides together.

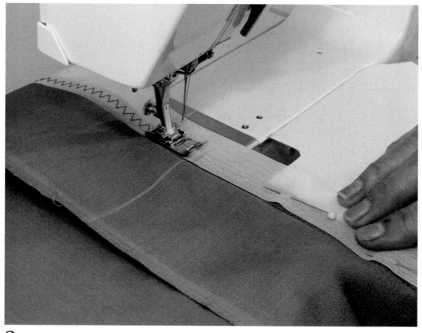

2 Attach Armoflexx to the seam allowance of the waistband with a wide zigzag stitch.

**Sew-in Waistbanding** A woven sew-in waistbanding known as Armoflexx creates a firm waistband and prevents the impression of the seam from showing. It's available by the yard in standard widths. The measurement and application of Armoflexx require a bit more care and skill than fusibles do.

Cut the interfacing to the same length as the waistband. Do not trim away the seam allowances. Even though it seems stiff, Armoflexx can be trimmed to almost nothing next to the seam to help stabilize the ends of the waistband. Transfer the markings.

Pin and stitch the waistband to the skirt with right sides together, matching the seams and centers and easing as needed (**1**). Press.

Match the corresponding side-seam and center marks on the interfacing and waistband. Position the edge of the interfacing next to the stitching line, pinning as needed, and stitch in the seam allowance. A wide, long zigzag stitch holds all layers flat (**2**). Press.

**Layered Interfacing** Both fusible and sew-in interfacings may be applied in single or double layers. I've had better results with fusibles. Sew-ins tend not to lie smooth and flat, but if you prefer to use them, here's what you would do.

Choose two layers of the same material or combine two different types. Although the construction principles are the same for both sew-in and fusible, the preliminary steps vary.

Cut the first layer of interfacing (on the lengthwise or cross grain if it is woven) to the same length as the waistband. Cut a second piece of interfacing on the bias to the same length and the finished width plus ¾ in. The bias-cut piece provides stability and softness, and will produce a stable waistband with a soft curve to its upper edge.

**Fusible:** Fuse the larger piece to the wrong side of the waistband. Now fuse the bias-cut piece on top of the larger, so the long front edge is ⅛ in. inside the stitching line of the waistband (**1**). This way, the second layer won't be caught in the stitching and ¾ in. will extend beyond the fold for a crisp edge. This technique is best for heavier fabrics; for lightweight fabrics, you can stitch through both layers of interfacing.

**Sew-in:** Hand- or machine-baste the larger piece to the wrong side of the front half of the waistband, ⅛ in. inside the stitching line. Baste the second layer to the first, stitching along the fold line and ⅛ in. inside all the seamlines (**2**). If you're using more than one layer of interfacing, trim the seam allowance in the top layer only.

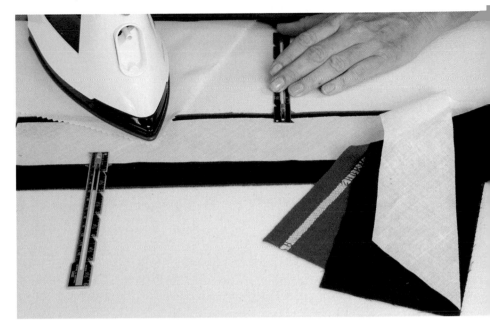

**1** *After fusing the first piece of interfacing, fuse the second smaller piece on top of it, inside the stitching line. Use a press cloth if necessary.*

**2** *Sew the waistband to the skirt.*

To add an extra bit of "crunch" to either the fusible or sew-in interfacing, machine-stitch two rows, ¼ in. apart, on the back half of the waistband, ¼ in. from the fold line.

# Fitted Elasticized Waistband

### Amount of Ease:

*Waistband length: Waist measurement plus 1 in. to 3 in. (plus 1¼ in. for two ⅝-in. seam allowances). Skirt waist: The waist seamline of the skirt should measure 1 in. to 3 in. more than the waistband measurement.*

A fitted elasticized waistband has style, comfort, and fit, too. It works with any skirt fabric, from crepe de chine to denim. Both the skirt and the waistband have a bit of extra ease, which the elastic draws in.

This waistband is perfect for figures with a small waist and high round hips. It has a slightly puckered, seersucker appearance when on the hanger, but is flattering on the body. The extra fabric hardly shows and adds no bulk. With this style of waistband, the skirt must have a zipper or a buttoned or side-pocket opening (p. 69).

***Cutting the Waistband*** Cut the waistband, adding 1 in. to 3 in. of ease to the length. The elastic will draw in the extra fabric. Mark the seams, centers, and underlap.

The waist seamline of the skirt should measure 1 in. to 3 in. more than your waistband measurement. Simply cut the waistband to your waist measurement plus 1 in. to 3 in., and then allow for seam and underlap allowances.

Cut the elastic to your waist measurement minus up to 3 in., plus seam allowances and underlap. I recommend Ban-rol elastic or flat-rib elastic, but if you plan to topstitch, use Ban-rol. The dense texture of flat-rib elastic makes it difficult to stitch through.

***Constructing the Waistband***
With right sides together, sew the long edge of the waistband to the skirt with a ⅝-in. seam allowance **(1)**. Press.

Mark the seam allowances, side seams, and front and back centers on the elastic. After you've sewn and pressed the first seam on the waistband, pin the elastic at the marked points, positioning the edge of the elastic next to the waistband stitching line.

Stitch the elastic to the waistband's seam allowance with a long, wide zigzag stitch **(2)**. Stretch the elastic

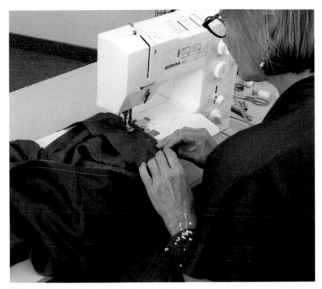

**1** *Sew the long edge of the waistband to skirt, right sides together.*

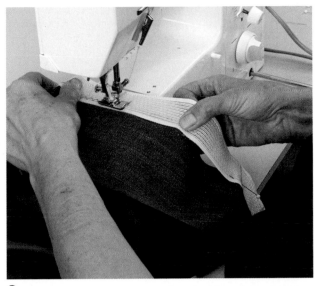

**2** *Sew the elastic to the waistband with a zigzag stitch.*

while stitching between the side seams, but not while stitching the underlap or the seam allowances at the ends.

Next, finish the ends of the waistband as described on p. 98. Trim, press, and turn.

Before the final stitching, to keep the top and bottom edges of the waistband flat, slip a small circle or square of fusible web (designed to fuse fabric together, and sold by the yard or in strips) between the back of the waistband and the elastic **(3)**. Press and fuse it in place. The elastic has a tendency to roll, and this technique is a bit of insurance to keep the top and bottom edges flat.

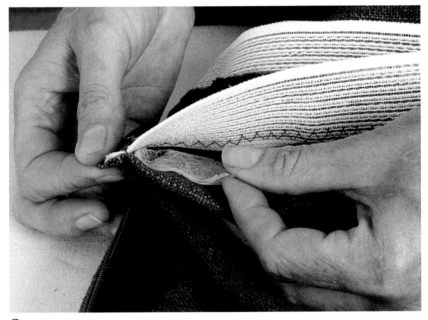

**3** *Insert and fuse fusible web between the elastic and the back of the waistband to keep the top and bottom edges flat.*

Cut and mark more than one length of elastic, and you'll save time when making your next waistband.

# FINISHING THE ENDS OF A WAISTBAND

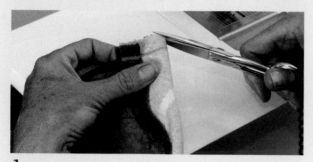

**1** *Mark the fold line with a snip on both ends of the waistband.*

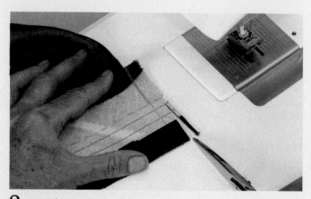

**2** *Trim ⅛ in. from the seam allowances at both ends of the inside half of the waistband. Trimming to the fold line "favors" the underside, which means that the ends will naturally roll to the underside of the waistband. Pin the waistband to hold it in position.*

**3** *Fold the waistband, right sides together, aligning the edges. Stitch across the waistband ends. Trim the corners, grade the seams, and trim the interfacing from the seam allowance. Press flat. Press open with a point turner.*

**4** *Turn the waistband with a point turner.*

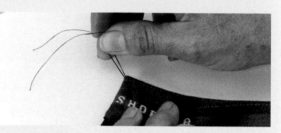

**5** *To turn the corner squarely, take a stitch by hand through the machine-stitching (with two strands of thread and no knot) and pull gently. Favor the seam to the underside, and press and pound with the clapper.*

**6** *On the right side, pin or hand-baste the waistband in place, catching both halves. Position the pins in the ditch of the seam so you can pull them out easily as you sew. Press the waistband as it will be sewn to make the final stitching easier and more accurate. On the right side of the garment, stitch in the ditch of the seam. Stitch the ends of the underlap together with a narrow zigzag or straight stitch. Be sure both halves of the underlap are caught in the stitching. Press over a ham to reinforce the natural curve of the waistband.*

# Contoured Waistband

**Amount of Ease:**

*Waistband length: Waist measurement plus 1 in. to 1½ in. (plus 1¼ in. for two ⅝-in. seam allowances). The waist seamline of the skirt should measure 1 in. to 1½ in. more than the waistband measurement.*

The ultimate in simplicity, the contoured waistband is very complimentary to short-waisted figures.The faced edge of the waistband sits precisely at the waistline, and the waistband facings fit the body's curves. The skirt of Chanel's classic suit—often of thick, nubby wool—has this waist finish, designed to lie smoothly beneath a silk shell.

A contoured waistband facing should measure 1 in. to 1½ in. larger than the finished waist measurement. Staystitch the waistline of the skirt ½ in. from the top edge.

Interface the waistband facings (pp. 93-95). Some body is desirable, but don't use interfacings that are too stiff. You don't need to trim away the interfacing in the seam allowances. Sew the seams, and trim the allowances to ¼ in. Finish the raw edge of the waistband facing with a Hong Kong finish, rayon seam binding, or serging.

Attach ¼-in. twill tape or a ¼-in. selvage strip from the lining fabric as you sew the facing to the skirt (**1**). This will prevent the

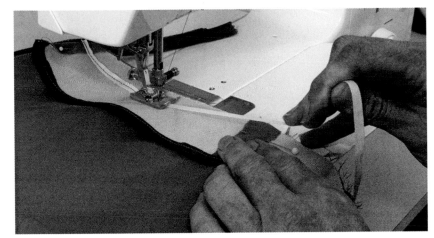

**1** *Sew the waistband facings to the skirt and reinforce them with twill tape or a strip of lining selvage.*

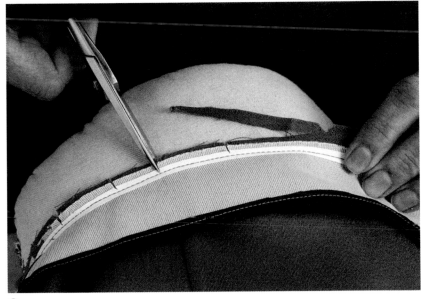

**2** *Grade and clip the stitched seams.*

facing from stretching as the garment is worn. You don't need to pin the tape in place first. As you stitch, ease the tape by pulling it slightly. Grade and clip the seams (**2**).

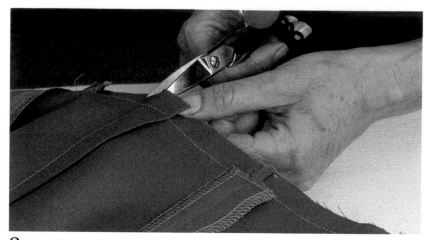

**3** Trim the excess fabric at the waistline so there aren't too many layers.

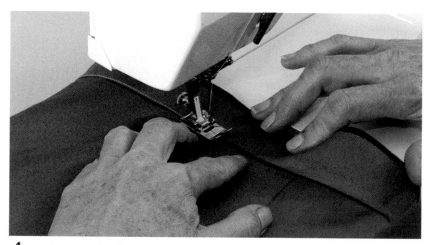

**4** Understitch the facing next to the seam. This helps the facing roll toward the inside of the skirt.

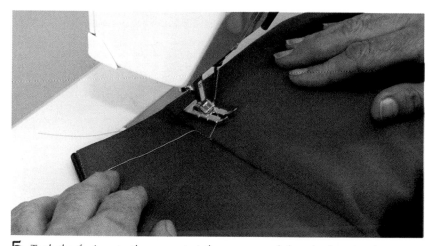

**5** Tack the facings to the garmet at the seams and darts by hand or by machine-stitching in the ditch on the right side of the garment.

Trim the excess fabric from the darts so there aren't too many layers of fabric at the waistline (**3**).

Press the seam flat, then press the seam allowances toward the facing. On the right side of the garment, with the facing extended away from the skirt, understitch the facing next to the seam (**4**). The understitching helps the facing roll toward the inside of the skirt. Press, favoring the facing to the wrong side.

Tack the facings to the garment at the seams and darts by hand or by machine-stitching in the ditch on the right side of the garment (**5**).

Turn under the ends of the facing next to the zipper and pin them. Slipstitch the facing to the zipper tape. Press the finished waistband over a ham to shape the contour.

### Converting to a Fitted Waist
You can convert the waist treatment of any fitted, darted skirt to a contoured waistband by eliminating the fitted waistband and making facing patterns.

Pin the darts on the front and back skirt-pattern pieces. Mark the pattern 3 in. from and parallel to the waistline edge. (With 5/8-in. seam allowances, the finished facing will be 2 3/8 in. wide.) Extend the skirt grainline on the facing areas and trace two separate facing pieces. Apply the contoured waistband facings as described.

# Raised Waistband

**Amount of Ease:**

*Waistband length: Waist measurement plus 1 in. at bottom of waistband; 1½ in. larger than midriff at top (plus 1¼ in. for two ⅝-in. seam allowances).*

A raised, or extended, waistband may extend from 1¼ in. to 3 in. higher than the natural waistline. It isn't separate from the garment, as are other kinds of waistbands; rather, it is cut as part of the skirt panels, then shaped with curves and darts and finished with a separate facing. This style is best for long-waisted figures without much waistline definition or a large bust.

One of the secrets to a crisp raised waistband is to interface the facing as well as the garment. Cut the skirt interfacing using the front and back skirt-pattern pieces, and follow the shaping at the top of the skirt. Cut the interfacing so it is ½ in. wider than the skirt facing. Fuse and position the pieces before marking and sewing darts and tucks.

Use a heavier weight of fusible or sew-in interfacing for the facing than for the skirt. It isn't necessary to trim interfacing in seam allowances.

**Boning** Keep the waistband from crushing or rolling down the waistline by adding boning. Boning, available under the brand name Rigiline, is sold by the foot. It is pliable, soft, easy to stitch through, and comfortable to wear, and it is available in black and white.

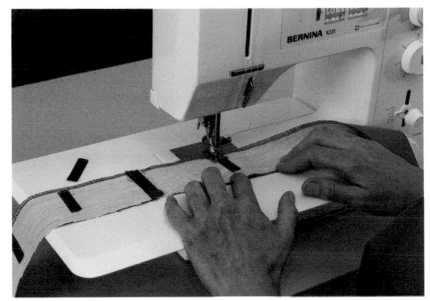

*Cut boning so that it fits just inside the seamlines on the facing, and stitch around each strip.*

Cut a piece of boning for each seam and dart to the height of the finished waistband, without seam allowances.

Sew the boning to the wrong side of the facing at center front and back, at the side seams, and halfway between the centers and side seams. Stitch around all sides of the boning strips (above).

Construct the facings, tape the edges, and attach the facings as you would for the contoured waistband (pp. 98-99).

Closures are optional for a high raised waistband or a contoured, faced waistband. Frequently closures for these waistband styles are omitted in ready-to-wear, but the classic recommendation is a fine metal hook and eye positioned under the zipper to add a bit of extra security.

# Hooks and Eyes

You can close a skirt with buttons, snaps, or hooks and eyes. Buttons are appropriate only if you've used a lightweight interfacing in the waistband—it's difficult to make a good buttonhole through the many layers and uneven thickness at the ends of most waistbands. Snaps have a tendency to pop open under pressure, so they aren't a good choice either. Large hooks and eyes are the most practical hidden fasteners for the overlapping edges on waistbands. They're flat enough to avoid bulk and strong enough to hold up to the firm interfacings and beefy elastics that most waistbands require.

You'll need two sets of hooks and eyes designed for waistbands. Use black metal with dark fabric colors, silver with light.

Hand-sew the first hook ¼ in. from the edge of the waistband overlap (**1**). With two strands of waxed thread, make small, short stitches next to each other, or use a blanket stitch to form a series of knots to cover the metal. The stitching should not show on the right side of the waistband. Make two small knots in the last stitch to secure the stitching.

Finish by making a tailor's knot, or quilter's knot, in the thread ½ in. from the surface of the fabric. Take a 1-in. stitch next to the hook, between the layers, and tug the thread to bury the knot. Trim the thread end where it emerges from the fabric.

The positon of the first hook determines the position of the corresponding eye. Eyes may be sewn on by hand or machine.

To sew eyes by machine, drop the feed dogs and attach a buttonhole foot (**2**). Adjust the width of the zigzag to clear the metal and make about 10 stitches through the eye. Finish by positioning the needle in the hole, adjust the stitch, and take three to four stitches in place.

Close the first hook and eye so the waistband is curved, as it will be when worn. Mark and sew the second hook about ½ in. from the edge of the underlap (depending on the length of the underlap) and position the second eye (**3**). This innermost closure bears most of the stress. Allow a slight bit of slack in the waistband between the first and second sets of closures.

**1** *Attach the first hook with a series of stitches made with waxed thread.*

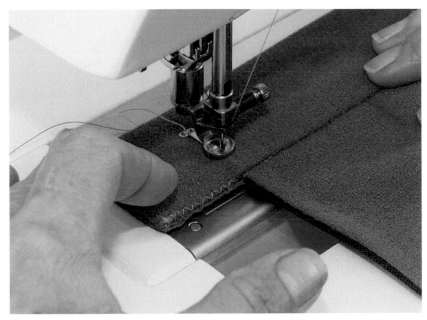

**2** *Attach the eyes with zigzag stitches, using a buttonhole foot.*

**3** *Install two sets of hooks and eyes in the waistband for extra strength. The innermost closure bears most of the stress.*

# Hemming the Skirt

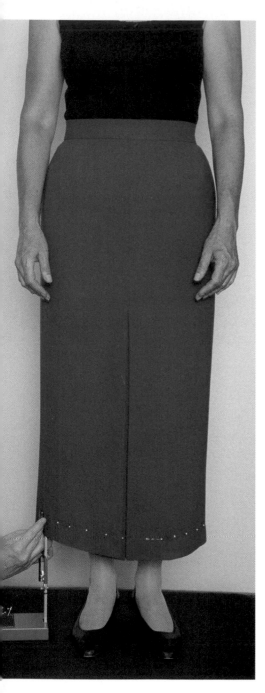

*The hem adds the finishing touch to a skirt. The type of hem you make, its width, and whether you sew it by hand or machine depends upon the fabric, style, and overall design of the skirt.*

The overall effect of the finished hem should be smooth and fluid. The edge needs to be even and parallel to the floor. You can sew a hem by hand or machine, but hand-stitching should be invisible and machine-stitching and topstitching must be straight.

## Hem Width

The hem width on the pattern piece provides a guideline, but always consider the style of the skirt and the fabric when deciding on hem width. The fabric is really the deciding factor. Some soft fabrics ease well; some firm fabrics may not.

A straight skirt generally requires a 2-in. to 2½-in. hem. Patterns often recommend ⅝-in. machine-topstitched hems for flared skirts. However, a narrow hem may roll to the outside. A slightly wider hem (¾ in. to ⅞ in.) may hang better and is just as easy to make. I prefer flared skirts with hems as wide as 1½ in. to 1⅝ in.

The wider the flare of the skirt, however, the smaller you should make the hem. A smaller hem has less fabric to ease.

Easing in the raw edge on a flared or shaped skirt prevents the formation of little tucks or pleats that may show through on the right side. Staystitch-plus (p. 60) with a standard straight stitch or use a serger with differential feed to ease and finish the raw edge in one operation.

## Marking

For accuracy, it's best to have tanother person mark the hem. The helper should move around the person being measured so the garment won't shift.

Determine the length you want the finished garment to be (p. 28). Mark the finished length with a hem marker or a yardstick that has been marked with a piece of masking tape as a guide. Place pins parallel to the floor every 2 in. to 3 in. Pin the front section of the hem to make sure the length is right and double-check the pin positions.

Remove the skirt. Press the hem under, along the pins, removing them as you come to them. Don't try to press to the exact placement of the pins—simply use them to determine a smooth, straight line. Then pin the hem up and try on the skirt again. Adjust the hem as needed.

Measure with a seam gauge, mark the hem to an even width with chalk, and trim evenly along the marked line (**1**). (Or you can simply serge along the marked line). Trim the seam allowances within the hem to $\frac{1}{4}$ in. to eliminate unnecessary bulk (**2**). Finish the raw edge, as described on p. 107.

Press the hem in place by carefully pressing the bottom two-thirds of the hem. This will keep the hem from showing through on the right side of the garment.

**1** *Mark the hem and trim evenly along the marked line.*

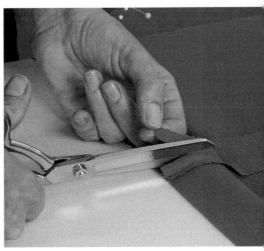

**2** *Trim the seam allowances within the hem to $\frac{1}{4}$ in.*

# Hemming by Hand

Hand-sewing hems creates softer, less obvious hems, which are particularly well suited for dressier skirts. Some fabrics, like silk, tend to shift, stretch, or distort when machine-stitched, and they're easier to control if they're hemmed by hand.

Silk thread or a long-staple polyester thread are both nearly invisible when stitched. Cotton thread is fine for midweight garments. Use as fine a needle as you can see to thread and a short length of a single strand. The end knot should be just to your elbow when the needle is threaded and ready to sew.

Secure and bury the knot in a seam. Fold the edge of the hem back $\frac{1}{4}$ in. and stitch along this fold. This prevents the stitches from showing.

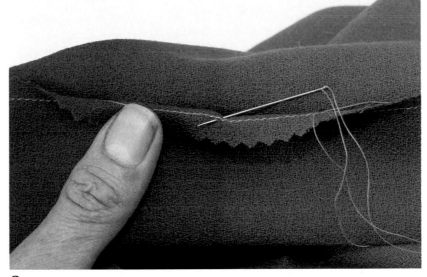

**3** *Hem by hand with loose stitches, catching just a fiber of the fabric, and make knots every 4 in. to 6 in.*

Catch just a fiber of the fabric as you stitch (don't worry, it will hold). Make loose stitches $\frac{1}{4}$ in. to $\frac{3}{8}$ in. long and form a knot every 4 in. to 6 in. (**3**). Loose stitches won't show through; the knots ensure that the hem will stay up even if a few stitches should get pulled out during normal wear-and-tear.

## HEMMING RIPPLE-FREE

Woven fabric is on the cross grain around a hem (and to further complicate things, sometimes it's off bias, too), so it can stretch, pucker, and ripple while you're machine-stitching. To avoid these problems, try these tricks.

1. Stitch with "straight assurance," that is, hold the fabric taut and firm as it feeds through the machine so that the fabric doesn't stretch or ripple. Don't pull the fabric or stop the normal stitching action. (This does not work on knits.)

2. With both hands, pull the fabric at right angles to the needle as it feeds through the machine. This may also help reduce rippling and stretching of the top layer of fabric.

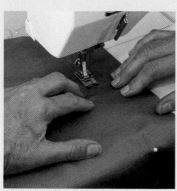

*Apply slight tension to each side of the stitching line.*

# Hemming by Machine

Fine ready-to-wear garments and commercial patterns are using machine-stitched and machine-topstitched hems more frequently. I use them for casual or sporty skirts.

***A Machine-Stitched Hem*** On silky or sheer fabrics, you can get good results with a minimum of frustration by machine-stitching a narrow hem. (Many sewers refer to this as a Calvin Klein hem because it shows up so often in the designer's line.) This hem features three lines of stitching and ensures a clean edge. It works on both the straight grain or bias and is a good choice for skirts in silk crepe de chine, georgette, and chiffon.

On the right side of the fabric, staystitch just within the marked finished hemline. Press along the stitched line. Now switch to an edgestitch foot and two-ply machine-embroidery thread, which is very fine and light.

Position the needle to the left of center and, with the fabric fold against the guide, stitch along the very edge of the underside of the hem. Trim the fabric as close to the stitching as possible with appliqué scissors. Press the fold under slightly—just enough to enclose the raw edge and create as narrow a hem as possible—and edgestitch the hem again on the right side.

A successful hem will have one line of stitching on the right side of the garment and two parallel lines of stitching on the hem. The line of

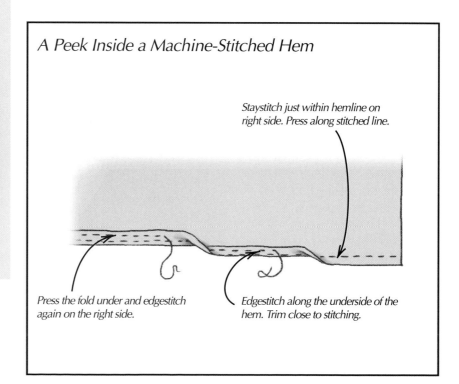

*A Peek Inside a Machine-Stitched Hem*

*Staystitch just within hemline on right side. Press along stitched line.*

*Press the fold under and edgestitch again on the right side.*

*Edgestitch along the underside of the hem. Trim close to stitching.*

staystitching will be enclosed within the fold. Press the garment on the right side.

**Hemming Knits** Knits demand the durability of a topstitched hem, but the hem can be frustrating to sew because knits stretch more on the cross grain.

Cut a ½-in. strip of bias-cut fusible tricot, such as Sof-Knit. Stitch it to the raw hem edge, wrong side of fabric to right side of fusible (the smooth side is the right side; you'll be sewing with the adhesive side up) **(1)**. On flared skirts, or if the knit is unstable or very stretchy, pull the interfacing strip to stretch it slightly as you stitch. You can also sew in this strip as you serge.

If you haven't serged them, pink the edges close to the line of stitching **(2)**. Fuse the hem into place, positioning it carefully. To secure and finish the hem, topstitch on the right side of the garment using staystitch plus as needed **(3)**.

# Final Pressing

Working on the wrong side of the garment, press the entire skirt and hem. Press only along the bottom edge of the hem, not across its full width—otherwise the impression of the hem might show through to the right side. Touch-up press on the right side of the garment, using a press cloth if necessary.

**1** *To stabilize a knit hem, stitch a strip of bias-cut fusible tricot to the raw edge.*

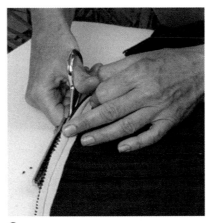

**2** *Pink close to the line of stitching.*

**3** *Topstitch the fused edge to keep it permanently in position.*

## SIX HEM FINISHES

The best hem finish is one that prevents fraying, yet is so light that it does not add bulk or show from the right side of the garment.

If you own a serger, the **serged edge** (p. 55) is a good finish for both hand- and machine-stitched hems. For a lighter finish, serge with machine-embroidery thread or woolly nylon.

Make a **pinked-and-stitched edge** (p. 54) by stitching ⅜ in. from the raw edge of the hem and trimming as little as possible with pinking shears or the pinking blade on a rotary cutter. You can also combine pinking with staystitch-plus (p. 60).

The **Hong Kong finish** or **rayon seam binding** (p. 56) is best for midweight to heavyweight fabrics. These edge finishes add bulk and may show through to the right side of lighter fabrics. Always test first.

The **turned-and-stitched edge** is suitable for midweight fabrics and crisp sheers with deep topstitched hems. It's also durable and therefore good for skirts that will be laundered.

The **zigzag edge** (p. 55) is fast to make and prevents raveling, but it can add bulk and cause the fabric to tunnel or stretch. For best results, stitch ¼ in. from the raw edge and trim after stitching. It's good for midweight to heavyweight fabrics, casual wear, and children's clothes.

# Test Your Skills: A Gored Skirt

*The gored skirt is a true classic—chic and flattering and always in style. Now that you know the many tricks of the trade, try out your professional skirtmaking skills with this easy-to-sew skirt.*

A gored skirt combines the lines of a slim and flared skirt, may be fitted or full, is flattering to almost any size and shape, is comfortable to wear, and easy to fit and sew.

Gored skirts can be shaped in various ways (p.12). The fullness may begin at the waist, the high hip, the full hip, or below the hip.

Choose the fabric weight according to the fit. The most fitted gored skirts are best in fabrics with weight and drape, such as gabardine or wool crepe, or a stable, heavier knit, such as wool double knit or velour. The fullest gored skirts are best in very lightweight fabrics, such as challis and light, fine knits.

In many commercial patterns, the gores are often the same size—for example, you would cut the same pattern piece eight times for an eight-gore skirt. In multiple-size patterns, the extra amounts for the size increments are added to the side panels.

Both fitted and full gored skirts can be seamed on the serger or on a standard sewing machine. Use a separate pull-on waistband and hem by hand or machine. Here are some tips for constructing a lightly fitted, fitted, or full gored skirt.

## Tips for a Lightly Fitted Gored Skirt

The silhouette of a lightly fitteed gored skirt is similar to a straight skirt, but it allows more ease in movement. It's also slimming and very flattering to a large-hipped figure.

Short to ankle-grazing lengths work well with this style.

Use a commercial pattern for a six- or eight-gore skirt and a heavy, stable, knit fabric—wool double knit, velour, panné velvet, or heavy cotton double knit, for example.

The trick is to cut the pattern two to three sizes larger than your body measurements (p. 28). The heavy knit drags and stretches, so you want extra width to give the illusion of fit, yet enough ease so that the skirt appears to float over the body.

Use standard seams with wool double knit (no other finish is necessary); serged or stitched and zigzag seams with velour or panné, which tends to curl.

Stitch the front and back sections of the skirt together first and adjust the fit at the side seams. The skirt should pull on easily over the hips, so use a pull-on elasticized waistband (pp. 89-91). Hand-stitch (p. 105) or machine-topstitch (p. 106) the hem.

Stitch the side seams last. Before you do, however, pin along the seamlines, wrong sides together. Try on the skirt and adjust the seam width as needed to get the best fit.

# Tips for a Fitted Gored Skirt

Making a fitted fored skirt is the most time-comsuming and difficult of the three possible styles. It is fitted at both the waist and the hip. You can find four-, six-, and eight-gore patterns in this style. The skirt works well in both short and long lengths.

Fit and alter the pattern carefully, allowing the correct amount of ease (p. 32).

Wool crepe or gabardine is a good fabric choice. Sew a standard seam with the edges serged or pinked (p. 54).

This is the perfect opportunity to use an invisible zipper at the center back or on a side seam (pp. 80-81). Apply a classic, fitted waistband (pp. 92-93) or a fitted elasticized waistband (pp. 96-97).

# Tips for a Full Gored Skirt

A full, ten-gore skirt is fast and foolproof to make, and very slimming. Cut this style so it is long and dramatic: a 32-in. to 35-in. finished length is average.

The finished skirt is full, but not bulky at the waist and hip. Use a lightweight knit, such as wool jersey, rayon, and Lycra blend; thin, drapey wovens; silk crepe; or the finest challis.

Use any eight-gore skirt pattern in your size. Cut ten gores instead of eight—five for the front and five for the back. (Buy one extra length of fabric to accommodate the two additional gores.)

Serge all the seams (p. 55) or straight-stitch and zigzag (p. 55) or pink (p. 54) the edges. No fitting is necessary. Apply a pull-on, elasticized waistband (pp. 89-91).

Mark the hem, and stitch it by hand or by machine (pp. 105-106). Topstitch if your skirt is made of a knit fabric.

# Index